SAY IT IN FRENCH

BY

LEON J. COHEN

GOSHEN CENTRAL SCHOOL
GOSHEN, N.Y.

NEW YORK
DOVER PUBLICATIONS, INC.

Published in Canada by General Publishing Company, Ltd., 30 Lesmill Road, Don Mills, Toronto, Ontario.

Published in the United Kingdom by Constable and Company, Ltd., 10 Orange Street, London WC 2.

Standard Book Number: 486-20803-6

Library of Congress Catalog Card Number: 55-13819

Manufactured in the United States of America
Dover Publications, Inc.
180 Varick Street
New York, N. Y. 10014

TABLE OF CONTENTS

SCHEME OF PRONUNCIATION

The difficulties of pronunciation of French for an American arise mainly from the difference in the pronunciation of vowels. English vowels are usually not one sound, but two; French vowels are pure, consisting of one sound only. Remember not to drawl them as in English.

The pronunciation given should be read simply as in English, with the stress placed slightly at the end of each word or group of words. When the pronunciation is in capitals, stress the capitalized syllable. Since in some cases the pronunciation of a group of letters differs according to the English word in which it is found and since a few French sounds cannot be represented in English, the following rules should be remembered:

ah—a broad *a*, as in *hard*.

ay—as in *say*.

aw—as in *saw*.

ee—as in *bee*.

eh—as the *e* in *let*.

ew—pucker your lips as if to kiss somebody and say *ee*; this sound is approximated in the English word *dew*.

g—always hard as the *g* in *go*.

zh—always soft as the *s* in *pleasure*.

oh—as in *blow*.

r—the French *r* is the sound made when one gargles.

s—always as in *sister*.

y—as in *yes*—never as in *my*.

The nasal sounds $\overline{ahn}$, $\overline{awn}$, $\overline{en}$, $\overline{uhn}$ are indicated by a line over the phonetic spelling. If these syllables are uttered "through the nose," the result will be adequate. Try pronouncing these syllables a few times while holding your nose. Then imitate these sounds. Be sure not to pronounce the *n*.

Although there are some regional differences, if you follow the pronunciation in this book, you will be understood.

NOTE: In order to facilitate the revision of this book, the publishers have skipped numbers from time to time. These do not indicate omissions in the text of the present edition.

USEFUL EXPRESSIONS
EXPRESSIONS UTILES

1. Yes. No. Perhaps.
Oui. Non. Peut-être.
wee. nawn. puh-TEH-truh.

2. Please. Excuse me.
S'il vous plaît. Excusez-moi.
seel voo pleh. ehx-kew-zay-mwah.

3. Thanks (very much).
Merci (beaucoup).
mehr-see (boh-koo).

4. You are welcome.
De rien.
duh ree-en.

5. I speak only English (French).
Je parle seulement anglais (français).
zhuh parl suhl-mahn ahn-gleh (frahn-seh).

6. German. Italian.
Allemand. Italien.
al-mahn. ee-tah-lyen.

7. I am from the United States.
Je viens des États-Unis.
zhuh vee-en day zay-ta-zew-nee.

8. My (mailing) address is ——.
Mon adresse (pour le courrier) est ——.
maw na-drehs (poor luh koor-yay) eh ——.

5

9. Please speak more slowly.
Veuillez parler plus lentement.
vuh-yay par-lay plew lahnt-mahn.

10. I (do not) understand.
Je (ne) comprends (pas).
zhuh (nuh) kawn-prahn (pa).

11. Repeat it, please.
Répétez-le, s'il vous plaît.
ray-pay-tay-luh, seel voo pleh.

12. Again.   Also.
Encore.   Aussi.
ahn-kawr.   oh-see.

13. Write it down, please.
Écrivez-le, s'il vous plaît.
ay-kree-vay-luh, seel voo pleh.

14. What do you wish?
Que voulez-vous?
kuh voo-lay-voo?

15. How much is it?
Combien est-ce?
kawn-byen ehss?

16. Come here.   Come in.
Venez ici.   Entrez.
vuh-nay zee-see.   ahn-tray.

17. Wait a moment.
Attendez un moment.
ah-tahn-day zuhn maw-mahn.

18. Why? When?
Pourquoi? Quand?
poor-kwah? kahn?

19. How? How long?
Comment? Combien de temps?
kaw-mahn? kawn-byen duh tahn?

20. How far? Who? What?
À quelle distance? Qui? Quoi?
ah kehl dees-tahns? kee? kwah?

21. Where is (are) ——?
Où est (sont) ——?
oo eh (sawn) ——?

22. The men's room. The ladies' room.
Hommes. Dames. *or* La toilette (for either).
awm. dahm. la twah-leht.

23. Here. There.
Ici. Là.
ee-see. la.

24. It is (it is not) all right.
C'est (ce n'est pas) bien.
seh (suh neh pas) byen.

25. It is old (new).
C'est vieux (nouveau).
seh vyuh (noo-voh).

26. Empty. Full.
Vide. Plein.
veed. plen.

27. That is (that is not) all.
C'est (ce n'est pas) tout.
seh (suh neh pah) too.

28. To. From. With.
À. De. Avec.
a. duh. a-vehk.

29. In. On. Near. Far.
Dans. Sur. Près de. Loin de.
dahn. sewr. preh duh. lwen duh.

30. In front of. Behind.
Devant. Derrière.
duh-vahn. deh-ryehr.

31. Beside. Inside. Outside.
À côté de. À l'intérieur. À l'extérieur.
ah koh-tay duh. ah len-tay-ryuhr. ah lehx-tay-ryuhr.

32. Something. Nothing.
Quelque chose. Rien.
kehl-kuh shohz. ree-en.

33. Several. Few.
Plusieurs. Quelques.
plew-zyuhr. kehl-kuh.

34. (Much) more, less.
(Beaucoup) plus, moins.
(boh-koo) plew, mwen.

35. (A little) more, less.
(Un peu) plus, moins.
(uhn puh) plew, mwen.

36. Enough. Too much.
Assez. Trop.
a-say. troh.

37. Much. Many.
Beaucoup. Beaucoup.
boh-koo. boh-koo.

38. Good. Better (than).
Bon. Meilleur (que).
bawn. may-yuhr (kuh).

39. Bad. Worse (than).
Mauvais. Pire (que).
moh-veh. peer (kuh).

40. Now. Immediately.
Maintenant. Tout de suite.
ment-nahn. toot sweet.

41. Soon. Later.
Bientôt. Plus tard.
byen-toh. plew tahr.

42. As soon as possible.
Aussitôt que possible.
oh-see-toh kuh paw-SEE-bluh.

43. At the latest. At least.
Au plus tard. Au moins.
oh plew tahr. oh mwen.

44. It is (too) late.
C'est (trop) tard.
seh (troh) tahr.

45. It is early.
C'est tôt.
seh toh.

46. Slowly.   Slower.
Lentement.   Plus lentement.
lahnt-mahn.   plew lahnt-mahn.

47. Quickly.   Faster.
Vite.   Plus vite.
veet.   plew veet.

48. I am (not) in a hurry.
Je (ne) suis (pas) pressé.
zhuh (nuh) swee (pah) preh-say.

49. I am warm (cold).
J'ai chaud (froid).
zhay shoh (frwah).

50. I am hungry (thirsty, sleepy).
J'ai faim (soif, sommeil).
zhay fen (swahf, saw-may).

51. I am busy (tired, ill, lost).
Je suis occupé (fatigué, malade, perdu).
zhuh swee zaw-kew-pay (fa-tee-gay, ma-lad, pehr-dew).

52. What is the matter here?
Qu'y a-t-il?
kee a teel?

53. Help!   Fire!   Thief!
Au secours!   Au feu!   Au voleur!
oh suh-koor!   oh fuh!   oh vaw-luhr!

54. Look out!
Attention!
ah-tahn-syawn.

55. Listen.   Look here.
Écoutez.   Regardez.
ay-koo-tay.   ruh-gar-day.

56. Can you help me (tell me)?
Pouvez-vous m'aider (me dire) ——?
poo-vay voo may-day (muh deer) ——?

57. I am looking for ——.
Je cherche ——.
zhuh shehrsh ——.

58. I should like ——.
Je voudrais ——.
zhuh voo-dreh ——.

59. Can you recommend a ——?
Pouvez-vous me recommander un ——?
poo-vay voo muh ruh-kaw-mahn-day uhn ——?

60. Do you want ——?
Voulez-vous ——?
voo-lay voo ——?

61. I am glad.   I am sorry.
J'en suis content.   Je regrette.
zhahn swee kawn-tahn.   zhuh ruh-greht.

62. It is (it is not) my fault.
C'est (ce n'est pas) ma faute.
seh (suh neh pah) ma foht.

63. Whose fault is it?
  À qui la faute?
  ah kee la foht?

64. I (do not) know.
  Je (ne) sais (pas).
  zhuh (nuh) say (pah).

65. I (do not) think so.
  Je (ne) le crois (pas).
  zhuh (nuh) luh krwah (pah).

66. What is that for?
  À quoi ça sert-il?
  ah kwah sa sehr-teel?

67. What is this called in French?
  Comment appelle-t-on ceci en français?
  kaw-mahn tah-pehl-tawn suh-see ahn frahn-seh?

68. How do you say ——?
  Comment dit-on ——?
  kaw-mahn dee-tawn ——?

69. How do you spell ⌈write⌉ ——?
  Comment écrivez-vous ——?
  kaw-mahn tay-kree-vay-voo ——?

DIFFICULTIES
DIFFICULTÉS

72. I cannot find my hotel address.
  Je ne peux pas trouver l'adresse de mon
  hôtel.
  *zhuh nuh puh pah troo-vay la-drehs duh maw
  noh-tehl.*

73. I do not remember the street.
Je ne me rappelle pas la rue.
zhuh nuh muh ra-pehl pah la rew.

74. I have lost my friends.
J'ai perdu mes amis.
zhay pehr-dew meh za-mee.

75. I left my purse (wallet) in the ——.
J'ai laissé mon sac (portefeuille) dans le
——.
zhay leh-say mawn sak (pawrt-fuh-yuh) dahn luh
——.

76. I forgot my money (keys).
J'ai oublié mon argent (mes clés).
zhay oo-blee-ay maw nar-zhahn(may klay).

77. I have missed my train (plane, bus).
J'ai manqué mon train (avion, autobus).
*zhay mahn-kay mawn tren (av-yawn, oh-taw-
bews).*

78. What am I to do?
Que dois-je faire?
kuh DWAH-zhuh fehr?

79. You said it would cost ——.
Vous avez dit qu'il coûterait ——.
voo za-vay dee keel koot-reh ——.

80. They are bothering me.
Ils m'ennuient.
eel mahn-nwee.

81. Go away.
Allez-vous-en.
a-lay-voo-zahn.

82. I will call a policeman.
Je vais appeler un agent.
zhuh vay za-play uh na-zhahn.

83. Where is the police station?
Où est le commissariat de police?
oo eh luh kaw-mee-sa-rya duh paw-leess?

84. I have been robbed of ——.
On m'a volé ——.
awn ma vaw-lay ——.

85. The lost and found desk.
Le bureau des objets trouvés.
luh bew-roh day zawb-zheh troo-vay.

GREETINGS AND INTRODUCTIONS
SALUTATIONS ET PRÉSENTATIONS

88. Good morning.   Good evening.
Bonjour.   Bonsoir.
bawn-zhoor.   bawn-swahr.

89. Hello.   Good-bye.
Bonjour.   Au revoir.
bawn-zhoor.   awr-vwahr.

90. I'll be seeing you.
À bientôt.
ah byen-toh.

91. My name is.
Je m'appelle ——.
zhuh ma-pehl ——.

92. What is your name?
Comment vous appelez-vous?
kaw-mahn voo zap-play voo?

93. May I introduce Mr. (Mrs., Miss) ——?
Puis-je présenter Monsieur (Madame, Mademoiselle) ——?
pwee-zhuh pray-zahn-tay muh-syuh (ma-dahm, mad-mwah-zehl) ——?

94. My wife. My husband.
Ma femme. Mon mari.
ma fahm. mawn ma-ree.

95. My daughter. My son.
Ma fille. Mon fils.
ma fee-uh. mawn feess.

96. My friend.
Mon ami.
maw na-mee.

97. My sister. My brother.
Ma sœur. Mon frère.
ma suhr. mawn frehr.

98. I am happy to make your acquaintance.
Je suis charmé de faire votre connaissance.
zhuh swee shahr-may duh fehr VAWT-ruh kawn-nehs-sahnss.

99. How are you?

Comment allez-vous?

kaw-mahn tal-lay-voo?

100. Fine, thanks.   And you?

Très bien, merci.   Et vous?

treh byen, mehr-see.   ay voo?

101. How is your family?

Comment va votre famille?

kaw-mahn va VAWT-ruh fa-mee-yuh?

102. (Not) very well.

(Pas) très bien.

(pah) treh byen.

103. Please sit down.

Veuillez vous asseoir.

vuh-yay voo za-swahr.

104. I have enjoyed myself very much.

Je me suis très bien amusé.

zhuh muh swee treh byeh nah-mew-zay.

105. I hope to see you again soon.

J'espère vous revoir bientôt.

zhess-pehr voo ruh-vwahr byen-toh.

106. Come to see me (us).

Venez me (nous) voir.

vuh-nay muh (noo) vwahr.

107. Give me your address (and tele-phone number).

Donnez-moi votre adresse (et votre numéro de téléphone).

daw-nay-mwah vaw-tra-drehss (ay VAW-truh new-may-roh duh tay-lay-fawn).

108. Give my regards to ——.

Mes amitiés à ——.

may za-mee-tyay za ——.

109. We are traveling to ——.

Nous voyageons à ——.

noo vwah-ya-zhawn za ——.

TRAVEL: GENERAL EXPRESSIONS
VOYAGE: EXPRESSIONS GÉNÉRALES

112. I want to go to the airline office.

Je veux aller au bureau de la compagnie
d'aviation.

*zhuh vuh zal-lay oh bew-roh duh la kawn-pan-
yee da-vee-ah-see-awn.*

113. The air port.   The bus station.

L'aérodrome.   La gare des autobus.

la-ay-raw-drohm.   la gar day zaw-toh-bewss.

114. The dock.   The railroad station.

Le quai.   La gare.

luh kay.   la gar.

115. How long will it take to go to ——?

Combien de temps le voyage à —— va-t-il
durer?

*kawn-byen duh tahn luh vwah-yazh a —— va-
teel dew-ray?*

116. When will we arrive at ——?

Quand arriverons-nous à ——?

kahn tah-ree-vuh-rawn-noo za ——?

117. Please get me a taxi.

Appelez-moi un taxi, s'il vous plaît.

ap-play-mwah uhn tak-see, seel voo pleh.

118. The ticket office.
Le guichet.
luh ghee-sheh.

119. A ticket.   A timetable.
Un billet.   Un horaire.
uhn bee-yeh.   uh-naw-rayr.

120. A porter.   The baggage room.
Un porteur.   La consigne.
uhn pawr-tuhr.   la kawn-SEEN-yuh.

121. The platform.
Le quai.
luh kay.

122. Is this seat taken?
Cette place est-elle prise?
seht plass eh-tehl preez?

123. Can I reserve a (front) seat?
Puis-je réserver une place (en avant)?
PWEE-zhuh ray-zehr-vay ewn plass (ah na-vahn)?

124. A seat near the window.
Une place près de la fenêtre.
ewn plass preh duh la fuh-NEH-truh.

125. Is this the (direct) way to ——?
Est-ce le chemin (direct) à ——?
ehs luh shuh-men (dee-rehkt) a ——?

126. How does one go (there)?
Comment va-t-on (là)?
kaw-mahn va-tawn (la)?

127. Where do I turn?
Où dois-je tourner?
oo DWAH-zhuh toor-nay?

128. To the north.   To the south.
Au nord.   Au sud.
oh nawr.   oh sewd.

129. To the west.   To the east.
À l'ouest.   À l'est.
ah lwehst.   ah lehst.

130. To the right.   To the left.
À droite.   À gauche.
ah drwaht.   ah gohsh.

131. Straight ahead.
Tout droit.
too drwah.

132. Forward.   Back.
En avant.   En arrière.
ah na-vahn.   ah na-ree-ehr.

133. Street.   Circle.   Place.
Rue.   Cercle.   Place.
rew.   SEHR-kluh.   plass.

134. Am I going in the right direction?
Est-ce la bonne direction?
ehs la bawn dee-rek-syawn?

135. Please point.
Voulez-vous me le montrer du doigt?
voo-lay-voo muh luh mawn-tray dew dwah?

136. What street is this?
Quelle est cette rue?
keh leh seht rew?

137. Do I have to change?
Dois-je changer?
DWAH-zhuh shahn-zhay?

138. Please tell me where to get off.
Veuillez me dire où il faut descendre.
vuh-yay muh deer oo eel foh day-SAHN-druh.

AT THE CUSTOMS
DOUANE

140. Where is the customs?
Où est la douane?
oo eh la doo-an?

141. Here is my baggage, —— pieces.
Voici mes bagages, —— pièces.
vwah-see may ba-gazh, —— pyehss.

142. Here is my passport (permit).
Voici mon passeport (permis).
vwah-see mawn pass-pawr (pehr-mee).

143. Must I open everything?
Dois-je tout ouvrir?
DWAH-zhuh too too-vreer?

144. I cannot open that.
Je ne peux pas l'ouvrir.
zhuh nuh puh pas loo-vreer.

145. I have lost my key.
J'ai perdu ma clé.
zhay pehr-dew ma klay.

146. I have nothing to declare.
Je n'ai rien à déclarer.
zhuh nay ree-eh na day-kla-ray.

147. All this is for my personal use.

Tout ceci est pour mon usage personnel.

too suh-see eh poor maw new-zazh pehr-saw-nehl.

148. There is nothing here but ——.

Il n'y a rien que —— ici.

eel nee a ree-en kuh —— ee-see.

149. These are gifts.

Ce sont des cadeaux.

suh sawn day ka-doh.

150. Are these things dutiable?

Ces choses sont-elles passibles des frais de douane?

say shohz sawn-tehl pa-SEE-bluh day freh duh doo-an?

151. How much must I pay?

Combien dois-je payer?

kawn-byen DWAH-zhuh pay-ay?

152. This is all I have.

C'est tout ce que j'ai.

seh too skuh zhay.

153. Please be careful.

Faites attention, s'il vous plaît.

feht za-tahn-syawn, seel voo pleh.

154. Have you finished?

Avez-vous fini?

a-vay voo fee-nee?

155. I cannot find my baggage.

Je ne peux pas trouver mes bagages.

zhuh nuh puh pah troo-vay may ba-gazh.

156. My train leaves in —— minutes.
    Mon train part dans —— minutes.
    mawn· tren par dahn —— mee-newt.

TICKETS
BILLETS

158. How much is a ticket to ——?
    Quel est le prix jusqu'à ——?
    kehl eh luh pree zhew-ska ——?

159. Where is the ticket office?
    Où est le guichet?
    oo eh luh ghee-sheh?

160. One-way (round trip) ticket.
    Un billet d'aller (d'aller et retour).
    uhn bee-yeh da-lay (da-lay ay ruh-toor).

161. First (second, third) class.
    Première (seconde, troisième) classe.
    pruh-myehr (suh-gawnd, trwa-zyem) klass.

162. Local.   Express.
    L'omnibus.   Le rapide.
    lawm-nee-bews.   luh ra-peed.

163. A reserved seat.
    Une place réservée.
    ewn plass ray-zehr-vay.

164. Can I go by way of ——?
    Puis-je y aller en passant par ——?
    pwee-zhee a-lay ahn pa-sahn par ——?

165. How long is this ticket good?
    Jusqu'à quand ce billet est-il valable?
    zhew-ska kahn suh bee-yeh eh teel va-LAH-bluh?

166. Can I get something to eat on the way?

Peut-on obtenir de quoi manger en route?

puh-tawn awp-tuh-neer duh kwah mahn-zhay ahn root?

167. How much baggage can I take?

Combien de kilos de bagages ai-je le droit d'emporter?

kawn-byen duh kee-loh duh bah-gazh AY-zhuh luh drawh dahn-pawr-tay?

168. How much per kilogram for excess?

Combien par kilo pour l'excédent?

kawn-byen par kee-loh poor lehk-say-dahn?

BAGGAGE
BAGAGES

170. Where is the baggage checked?

Où enregistre-t-on les bagages?

oo ahn-ruh-ZHEE-struh-tawn lay ba-gazh?

171. I want to leave these bags for a while.

Je veux laisser ces valises un peu.

zhuh vuh leh-say say va-leez uhn puh.

172. Do I pay now or later?

Dois-je payer maintenant ou plus tard?

DWAH-zhuh pay-yay ment-nahn oo plew tar?

173. I want to take out my baggage.

Je veux retirer mes bagages.

zhuh vuh ruh-tee-ray may ba-gazh.

174. That is mine there.
Voilà la mienne.
vwah-la la mee-ehn.

175. Handle this very carefully.
Faites attention avec celle-ci.
feht za-tahn-syawn a-vehk sehl-see.

TRAIN
CHEMIN DE FER

177. Where is the railroad station?
Où est la gare?
oo eh la gar?

178. I am going by train to ——.
Je prends le train pour ——.
zhuh prahn luh tren poor ——.

179. Is the train for —— on time?
Est-ce que le train pour —— est à l'heure?
ehs-kuh luh tren poor —— eh ta luhr?

180. It is —— minutes late.
Il a —— minutes de retard.
eel a —— mee-newt duh ruh-tar.

181. At what platform is the train for ——?
À quel quai est le train pour ——?
ah kehl kay eh luh tren poor ——?

182. Please put this in the rack.
Veuillez mettre ceci dans le filet.
vuh-yay MEH-truh suh-see dahn luh fee-leh.

183. Please open (close) the window.

Voulez-vous bien ouvrir (fermer) la fenêtre.

*voo-lay-voo byen oo-vreer (fehr-may) la fuh-
NEH-truh.*

184. Where is the diner (smoker)?

Où est le wagon-restaurant (fumeur) ?

oo eh luh va-gawn-rehs-taw-rahn (few-muhr)?

185. Do you mind my smoking?

Est-ce que la fumée vous incommode ?

ehs-kuh la few-may voo zen-kaw-mawd?

186. What time is (breakfast, lunch, dinner)?

À quelle heure sert-on le (petit déjeuner,
déjeuner, dîner) ?

*ah keh luhr sehr-tawn luh (puh-tee day-zhuh-nay,
day-zhuh-nay, dee-nay)?*

AIRPLANE
AVION

188. Is there a bus service to the airport?

Y a-t-il un service d'autobus pour l'aéro-
port ?

*ya tee luhn sehr-veess daw-taw-bewss poor la-ay-
raw-pawr?*

189. At what time will they come for me?

À quelle heure viendra-t-on me chercher ?

ah keh luhr vyen-dra-tawn muh shehr-shay?

190. When is there a plane to ——?

À quelle heure le vol pour —— ?

ah keh luhr luh vawl poor ——?

191. Is food served on the plane?

Peut-on obtenir de quoi manger à bord?

puh-tawn awp-tuh-neer duh kwah mahn-zhay ah bawr?

192. How many kilos may I take?

Combien de kilos puis-je apporter?

kawn-byen duh kee-loh PWEE-zhuh ah-pawr-tay?

BUS
AUTOBUS

194. Where is the bus station?

Où est la gare des autobus?

oo eh la gar day zaw-taw-bewss?

195. Can I buy an excursion ticket?

Puis-je prendre un billet d'excursion?

PWEE-zhuh PRAHN-druh uhn bee-yeh dehx-kewr-syawn?

196. Is there a stop for lunch?

Y a-t-il un arrêt pour le déjeuner?

ya tee luh na-reh poor luh day-zhuh-nay?

197. May I stop on the way?

Puis-je m'arrêter en route?

PWEE-zhuh ma-reh-tay ahn root?

BOAT
BATEAU

200. Can I go by boat to ——?

Puis-je aller par bateau à ——?

PWEE-zha-lay par ba-toh ah ——?

201. When does the next boat leave?
Quand le prochain bateau part-il?
kahn luh praw-shen ba-toh par-teel?

202. When must I go on board?
Quand dois-je embarquer?
kahn dwah zhahn-bar-kay?

203. Can I land at ——?
Pourrai-je débarquer à ——?
poor-ray-zhuh day-bar-kay ah ——?

204. The captain. The purser.
Le capitaine. Le commissaire.
luh ka-pee-tehn. luh kaw-mee-sayr.

205. The steward. The deck.
Le garçon. Le pont.
luh gar-sawn. luh pawn.

206. I want to rent a deck chair.
Je voudrais bien louer une chaise longue.
zhuh voo-dreh byen loo-ay ewn shehz lawng.

207. I am seasick.
J'ai le mal de mer.
zhay luh mal duh mehr.

208. I am going to my stateroom.
Je vais à ma cabine.
zhuh vay za ma ka-been.

209. Let's go (to the dining room, to the bar).
Allons (à la salle à manger, au bar).
a-lawn (zah la sal ah mahn-zhay, zoh bar).

210. A life boat.   A life preserver.

Un canot de sauvetage.   Une ceinture de sauvetage.

uhn ka-noh duh sohv-tazh.   ewn sen-tewr duh sohv-tazh.

AUTOMOBILE
AUTOMOBILE

215. Where is a gas station (garage)?

Où y a-t-il un poste d'essence (un garage)?

oo ya tee luhn pawst deh-sahnss (uhn ga-razh)?

216. Is the road good?

La route est-elle bonne?

la root eh tehl bawn?

217. Can you recommend a good mechanic?

Pouvez-vous m'indiquer un bon mécanicien?

poo-vay-voo men-dee-kay uhn bawn may-ka-nee-syen?

218. Is it paved or not?

Est-elle pavée ou pas?

eh-tehl pa-vay oo pah?

219. What town is this (the next one)?

Comment s'appelle cette ville (la prochaine)?

kawn-mahn sa-pehl seht veel (la praw-shehn)?

220. Where does that road go?

Où cette route va-t-elle?

oo seht root va-tehl?

221. The tourist club.
Le club touristique.
luh klewb too-rees-teek.

222. I have an international driver's licence.
J'ai un permis international.
zhay uhn pehr-mee en-tehr-na-syaw-nal.

223. I want some air.
Je veux de l'air.
zhuh vuh duh layr.

224. A map.
Une carte.
ewn kart.

225. How much is gas a liter?
Combien le litre d'essence?
kawn-byen luh LEE-truh deh-sahnss?

226. Give me —— liters.
Donnez-moi —— litres.
daw-nay-mwah —— LEE-truh.

227. Please change the oil.
Veuillez changer l'huile.
vuh-yay shahn-zhay lweel.

228. Light (medium, heavy) oil.
L'huile légère (moyenne, lourde).
lweel lay-zhehr (mwah-yehn, loord).

229. Put water in the battery.
Mettez de l'eau dans les accus.
meh-tay duh loh dahn lay za-kew.

230. Recharge it.
Rechargez-les.
ruh-shar-zhay-lay.

231. Will you lubricate the car?
Voulez-vous bien graisser la voiture?
voo-lay-voo byen greh-say la vwah-tewr?

232. Could you wash it now (soon)?
Pourriez-vous la laver maintenant (bientôt)?
poor-ryay-voo la la-vay ment-nahn (byen-toh)?

233. Tighten the brakes.
Resserrez les freins.
ruh-sehr-ray lay fren.

234. Will you check the tires?
Voulez-vous bien regarder les pneus?
voo-lay-voo byen ruh-gar-day lay pnuh?

235. Can you fix the flat tire?
Pouvez-vous réparer le pneu crevé?
poo-vay-voo ray-pa-ray luh pnuh kruh-vay?

236. A puncture. A slow leak.
Une crevaison.   Une légère fuite.
ewn kruh-vay-zawn.   ewn lay-zhehr fweet.

237. The —— does not work well.
Le —— ne marche pas bien.
luh —— nuh marsh pah byen.

238. What is wrong?
Qu'y a-t-il?
kee ah teel?

239. There is a grinding (leak, noise).
Il y a un grincement (une fuite, un bruit).
eel ya uhn grens-mahn (ewn fweet, uhn brwee).

240. The engine overheats.
Le moteur devient trop chaud.
luh maw-tuhr duh-vyen troh shoh.

241. The engine misses (stalls).
Le moteur rate (cale).
luh maw-tuhr raht (kal).

242. There is a rattle (squeak).
Il y a un cliquetis (un bruit aigu).
eel ya uhn kleek-tee (uhn brwee tay-gew).

243. May I park here for a while?
Puis-je stationner ici un peu?
PWEE-zhuh sta-syaw-nay ee-see uhn puh?

244. I want to garage my car for the night.
Je veux garer la voiture pour la nuit.
zhuh vuh ga-ray la vwah-tewr poor la nwee.

245. When does it open (close)?
À quelle heure est l'ouverture (la fermeture)?
ah keh luhr eh loo-vehr-tewr (la fehrm-tewr)?

PARTS OF THE CAR
MOTEUR ET CARROSSERIE

250. Accelerator. Battery.
L'accélérateur. Les accus.
lak-say-lay-ra-tuhr. lay-za-kew.

251. Bolt. Brake. Engine.
Le boulon. Le frein. Le moteur.
luh boo-lawn. luh fren. luh maw-tuhr.

252. Nut. Spring. Starter.
L'écrou. Le ressort. Le démarreur.
lay-kroo. luh ruh-sawr. luh day-mar-ruhr.

253. Steering wheel. Headlight.
Le volant. Le phare.
luh vaw-lahn. luh far.

254. Tail light. Tube. Tire.
Le feu arrière. La chambre à air. Le
    pneu.
*luh fuh ar-ryehr. la SHAHN-bra ayr. luh
    pnuh.*

255. Spare tire.
Le pneu de rechange.
luh pnuh duh ruh-shahnzh.

256. Wheel (front, back, left, right).
La roue (avant, d'arrière, gauche, droite).
la roo (ah-vahn, dar-ryehr, gohsh, drwaht).

TOOLS AND EQUIPMENT
OUTILS ET OUTILLAGE

260. Chains. Hammer. Jack.
Les chaînes. Le marteau. Le cric.
lay shehn. luh mar-toh. luh kreek.

261. Key. Pliers. Rope.
La clé. Les pinces. La corde.
la klay. lay penss. la kawrd.

262. Screwdriver.   Tire pump.   Wrench.
Le tourne-vis.   La pompe.   La clé.
luh toorn-veess.   la pawnp.   la klay.

HELP ON THE ROAD
AIDE SUR LA ROUTE

275. I am sorry to trouble you.
Je regrette de vous déranger.
zhuh ruh-greht duh voo day-rahn-zhay.

276. My car has broken down.
J'ai une panne.
zhay ewn pan.

277. Can you tow (push) me?
Pouvez-vous me remorquer (pousser)?
poo-vay-voo muh ruh-mawr-kay (poo-say)?

278. Can you help me jack up the car?
Pouvez-vous m'aider à lever la voiture avec
le cric?
*poo-vay-voo may-day ah luh-vay la vwah-tewr ah-
vehk luh kreek?*

279. Will you help me put on the spare?
Pouvez-vous m'aider à mettre la roue de
rechange?
*poo-vay-voo may-day ah MEH-truh la roo duh
ruh-shahnzh?*

280. Could you give me some gas?
Pouvez-vous me donner de l'essence?
poo-vay-voo muh daw-nay duh leh-sahnss?

281. Will you take me to a garage?
Voulez-vous bien m'amener à un garage?
voo-lay-voo byen mam-nay ah uhn ga-razh?

282. Will you help me get the car off the road?
Voulez-vous m'aider à retirer la voiture de la route?
voo-lay-voo may-day ah ruh-tee-ray la vwah-tewr duh la root?

283. My car is stuck in the mud.
Ma voiture est embourbée.
ma vwah-tewr eh tahn-boor-bay.

284. It is in the ditch.
Elle est dans le fossé.
eh leh dahn luh faw-say.

ROAD SIGNS AND PUBLIC NOTICES
AVIS

287. Aller. *al-lay.* **Go.**

288. Arrêtez. *ar-reh-tay.* **Stop.**

289. Attention. *ah-tahn-syawn.* **Drive carefully.**

290. Avertissez. *ah-vehr-tee-say.* **Sound your horn.**

291. Boulevard. *bool-var.* **Boulevard.**

292. Carrefour. *kar-foor.* **Intersection.**

293. Cassis. *ka-see.* **Dip.**

294. Croisement. *krwahz-mahn.* **Crossroads.**

295. Danger. *dahn-zhay.* **Danger.**

296. Défense de doubler.
day-fahns duh doo-blay.
No passing.

297. Défense d'entrer.
day-fahns dahn-tray.
No thoroughfare. **[Keep out.]**

298. Défense de fumer.
day-fahns duh few-may.
No smoking.

299. Deuxième vitesse.
duh-zyehm vee-tehss.
Use second gear.

300. École. *ay-kawl.* **School.**

301. Entrée. *ahn-tray.* **Entrance.**

302. Fermée. *fehr-may.* **Closed.**

303. Fils à haute tension.
feel ah oht tahn-syawn.
High tension lines.

304. Lentement. *lahnt-mahn.* **Slow.**

305. Passage à niveau.
pa-sazh ah nee-voh.
Railroad crossing.

306. Pente dangereuse.
pahnt dahn-zhuh-ruhz.
Steep grade.

307. Pont étroit (provisoire).
pawn ay-trwah (praw-vee-zwahr).
Narrow (temporary) bridge.

308. Ralentissez.
ra-lahn-tee-say.
Slow down.

309. Route étroite.
roo tay-trwaht.
Narrow road.

310. Route sinueuse.
root see-new-uhz.
Winding road.

311. Sens unique.
sahn sew-neek.
One way.

312. Sortie. *sawr-tee.* **Exit.**

313. Stationnement. *sta-syawn-mahn.* **Parking.**

314. Stationnement interdit.
sta-syawn-mahn en-tehr-dee.
No parking.

315. Tenez à droite.
tuh-nay za drwaht.
Keep right.

316. Tournant. *toor-nahn.* **Curve.**

317. Tournant double.
toor-nahn DOO-bluh.
Double curve.

318. Travaux. *tra-voh.* **Road repairs.**

319. Virage. *vee-razh.* **Sharp turn.**

320. Virage à droite (gauche) interdit.
vee-razh a drwaht (gohsh) en-tehr-dee.
No right (left) turn.

321. Vitesse   maximum —— kilomètres   à
l'heure.

*vee-tehs max-ee-muhm —— kee-law-MEH-truh
ah luhr.*

**Maximum speed —— kilometers per
hour.**

LOCAL BUS AND STREETCAR
AUTOBUS ET TRAMWAY

325. The bus stop.   The driver.
L'arrêt d'autobus.   Le conducteur.
lar-reh daw-taw-bewss.   luh kawn-dewk-tuhr.

326. What bus (car) do I take to ——?
Quel autobus (tramway) dois-je prendre
pour ——?
*keh law-taw-bewss (trahm-way) DWAH-zhuh
PRAHN-druh poor ——?*

**327. Where does the bus (car) for ——
stop?**
Où s'arrête l'autobus (le tramway) pour
——?
*oo sar-reht law-taw-bewss (luh trahm-way) poor
——?*

328. Do you go near ——?
Passez-vous près de ——?
pas-say-voo preh duh ——?

329. How much is the fare?
Combien?
kawn-byen?

330. A transfer, please.

Une correspondence, s'il vous plaît.

ewn kaw-rehs-pawn-dahns, seel voo pleh.

331. Off next stop, please.

Le prochain, s'il vous plaît.

luh praw-shen, seel voo pleh.

TAXI
TAXI

334. Please call a taxi for me.

Veuillez m'appeler un taxi.

vuh-yay map-lay uhn tak-see.

335. How far is it?

À quelle distance est-ce?

ah kehl deess-tahnss ehss?

336. How much will it cost?

Quel sera le prix?

kehl suh-ra luh pree?

337. That is too much.

C'est trop cher.

seh troh shehr.

338. What do you charge per hour (kilometer)?

Combien prenez-vous l'heure (le kilomètre)?

kawn-byen pruh-nay-voo luhr (luh kee-law-MEH-truh)?

339. I just wish to drive around.

Je veux simplement me promener en voiture.

zhuh vuh sen-pluh-mahn muh prawm-nay ahn vwah-tewr.

340. Please drive more slowly (carefully).

Veuillez conduire plus lentement (prudemment).

vuh-yay kawn-dweer plew lahnt-mahn (prew-da-mahn).

341. Stop here.   Wait for me.

Arrêtez ici.   Attendez-moi.

ar-reh-tay zee-see.   at-tahn-day-mwah.

342. How much do I owe?

Combien est-ce que je vous dois?

kawn-byen ehs kuh zhuh voo dwah?

THE HOTEL
HÔTEL

345. Which hotel is good (inexpensive)?

Connaissez-vous un bon hôtel (à prix modéré)?

kaw-neh-say-voo uhn baw noh-tehl (ah pree mawday-ray)?

346. The best hotel.

Le meilleur hôtel.

luh may-yuh roh-tehl.

347. Not too expensive.

Pas trop cher.

pah troh shehr.

348. I (do not) want to be in the center of town.

Je (ne) veux (pas) être au centre de la ville.

zhuh (nuh) vuh (pah) ZEH-truh oh SAHN-truh duh la veel.

349. Where it is not noisy.

Où il n'y a pas de bruit.

oo eel nee ah pah duh brwee.

350. I have a reservation for ——.

J'ai une réservation pour ——.

zhay ewn ray-zehr-va-syawn poor ——.

351. I want to reserve a room.

Je veux réserver une chambre.

zhuh vuh ray-zehr-vay ewn SHAHN-bruh.

352. I want a room with (without) meals.

Je désire une chambre avec (sans) repas.

zhuh day-zeer ewn SHAHN-bra vehk (sahn) ruh-pah.

353. I want a (single, double) room.

Je désire une chambre (à un lit, pour deux personnes).

zhuh day-zeer ewn SHAHN-bruh (ah uhn lee, poor duh pehr-sawn).

354. A room with a double bed.

Une chambre à grand lit pour deux.

ewn SHAHN-bra grahn lee poor duh.

355. A suite.   A bed.

Un appartement.   Un lit.

uh nap-par-tuh-mahn.   uhn lee.

356. With (bath, shower, twin beds).
Avec (salle de bain, douche, lits jumeaux).
a-vehk (sal duh ben̄, doosh, lee zhew-moh).

357. With a window (a balcony).
Avec une fenêtre (un balcon).
a-vehk ewn fuh-NEH-truh (uhn bal-kawn̄).

358. For —— days.   For tonight.
Pour —— jours.   Pour cette nuit.
poor —— zhoor.   poor seht nwee.

359. For —— persons.
Pour —— personnes.
poor —— pehr-sawn.

360. What is the rate per day?
Quel est votre prix par jour?
keh leh VAW-truh pree par zhoor?

361. Are tax and room service included?
Est-ce que les taxes et le service sont compris?
ehs-kuh lay tax ay luh sehr-veess sawn̄ kawn̄-pree?

362. A week.   A month.
Par semaine.   Par mois.
par suh-mehn.   par mwah.

363. On what floor?
À quel étage?
ah keh lay-tazh?

364. Upstairs.   Downstairs.
En haut.   En bas.
ahn̄ oh.   ahn̄ bah.

365. Is there an elevator?
Y a-t-il un ascenseur?
ya tee luh   na-sahn-suhr?

366. Running water.   Hot water.
L'eau courante.   L'eau chaude.
loh koo-rahnt.   loh shohd.

367. I want a room higher up.
Je désire une chambre à un étage plus
élevé.
*zhuh day-zeer ewn SHAHN-brah uh nay-tazh
plew zay-luh-vay.*

368. On a lower floor.
Plus bas.
plew bah.

369. I should like to see the room.
Je voudrais bien voir la chambre.
zhuh voo-dreh byen vwahr la SHAHN-bruh.

370. I (I do not) like this one.
J'aime (je n'aime pas) celle-ci.
zhehm (zhuh nehm pah) sehl-see.

371. Have you something better?
Avez-vous quelque chose de meilleur?
ah-vay-voo kehl-kuh shohz duh may-yuhr?

372. Cheaper.   Larger.   Smaller.
Moins cher.   Plus grand.   Plus petit.
mwen shehr.   plew grahn.   plew puh-tee.

373. With more light.   More air.
Avec plus de lumière.   Plus d'air.
a-vehk plew duh lew-myehr.   plew dayr.

374. I have baggage at the station.

J'ai mes bagages à la gare.

zhay may ba-gazh ah la gar.

375. Will you send for my bags?

Voulez-vous bien envoyer chercher mes
bagages?

*voo-lay-voo byen ahn-vwah-yay shehr-shay may
ba-gazh?*

376. Here is the check for my trunk.

Voici le bulletin d'enregistrement pour ma
malle.

*vwah-see luh bewl-ten dahn-reh-zheess-truh-
mahn poor ma mal.*

377. Please send —— to my room.

Faites monter —— dans ma chambre, s'il
vous plaît.

*feht mawn-tay —— dahn ma SHAHN-bruh,
seel voo pleh.*

378. Ice. Ice water.

La glace. L'eau glacée.

la glas. loh gla-say.

379. Please call me at —— o'clock.

Veuillez m'appeler à —— heures.

vuh-yay map-lay ah —— uhr.

380. I want breakfast in my room.

Je veux le petit déjeuner dans ma chambre.

*zhuh vuh luh puh-tee day-zhuh-nay dahn ma
SHAHN-bruh.*

381. Could I have some laundry done?
Puis-je faire laver des affaires?
PWEE-zhuh fehr la-vay day za-fehr?

382. I want some things pressed.
J'ai des choses à faire repasser.
zhay day shohz ah fehr ruh-pas-say.

383. I should like to speak to the manager.
Je voudrais bien parler au gérant.
zhuh voo-dreh byen par-lay oh zhay-rahn.

384. My room key, please.
Ma clé, s'il vous plaît.
ma klay, seel voo pleh.

385. Have I any letters or messages?
Y a-t-il des lettres ou des messages pour moi?
ya teel day LEH-truh·oo day mehs-sazh poor mwah?

386. What is my room number?
Quel est le numéro de ma chambre?
keh leh luh new-may-roh duh ma SHAHN-bruh?

387. I am leaving at —— o'clock.
Je pars à —— heures.
zhuh par ah —— uhr.

388. Please make out my bill.
Veuillez préparer ma note.
vuh-yay pray-pa-ray ma nawt.

389. May I store baggage here until ——?
Puis-je laisser des bagages ici jusqu'à ——?
PWEE-zhuh lehs-say day ba-gazh ee-see zhews-ka ——?

390. Please forward my mail to ——.

Veuillez faire suivre mon courrier à ——.

*vuh-yay fehr SWEE-vruh mawn koor-yay ah
——.*

CHAMBERMAID

FEMME DE CHAMBRE

393. Please open (close) the windows.

Veuillez ouvrir (fermer) les fenêtres.

vuh-yay zoov-reer (fehr-may) lay fuh-NEH-truh.

394. Do not disturb me until ——.

Ne me dérangez pas avant ——.

nuh muh day-rahn-zhay pah zah-vahn ——.

395. Please change the sheets today.

Veuillez changer les draps aujourd'hui.

vuh-yay shahn-zhay lay drah oh-zhoord-wee.

396. Bring me another blanket (pillow).

Apportez-moi encore une couverture (un
oreiller).

*ap-pawr-tay-mwah ahn-kawr ewn koo-vehr-tewr
(uh-naw-ray-yay).*

397. A pillow case. A bath mat.

Une taie d'oreiller. Un tapis de bain.

ewn tay daw-ray-yay. uhn ta-pee duh ben.

398. Hangers. A glass. The door.

Les cintres. Un verre. La porte.

lay SEN-truh. uhn vehr. la pawrt.

399. Soap.   Towels.   A candle.

Le savon.   Les serviettes.   Une bougie.

luh sa-vawn.   lay sehr-vee-eht.   ewn boozhee.

400. The bathtub.   The sink.

La baignoire.   Le lavabo.

la behn-ywahr.   luh la-va-boh.

401. Drinking water.   Toilet paper.

L'eau potable.   Le papier hygiénique.

loh paw-TA-bluh.   luh pap-yay ee-zhyay-neek.

See also COMMON OBJECTS, page 105.

402. Is there always hot water?

Y a-t-il toujours de l'eau chaude?

ya teel too-zhoor duh loh shohd?

403. Please come back later.

Veuillez revenir plus tard.

vuh-yay ruh-vuh-neer plew tar.

APARTMENT
APPARTEMENT

406. I want a furnished apartment.

Je désire un appartement meublé.

zhuh day-zeer uh nap-part-mahn muh-blay.

407. Living room.   —— bedrooms.

Un salon.   —— chambres.

uhn sa-lawn.   —— SHAHN-bruh.

408. A dining room.   A kitchen.

Une salle à manger.   Une cuisine.

ewn sal ah mahn-zhay.   ewn kwee-zeen.

409. A balcony.   A bathroom.
Un balcon.   Une salle de bain.
uhn bal-kawn.   ewn sal duh ben.

410. Is the linen furnished?
Est-ce qu'on fournit le linge ?
ehs-kawn foor-nee luh lenzh ?

411. How much is it a month?
Quel est le loyer par mois ?
keh leh luh lwah-yay par mwah ?

412. Blankets.   The silver.   Dishes.
Les couvertures.   L'argenterie.   La vais-
selle.
lay koo-vehr-tewr.   lar-zhahn-tree.   la veh-sehl.

413. Do you know a good cook?
Connaissez-vous une bonne cuisinière ?
kaw-neh-say-voo ewn bawn kwee-zee-nyehr ?

414. Where can I rent a garage?
Où puis-je louer un garage ?
oo PWEE-zhuh loo-ay uhn ga-razh ?

RESTAURANT AND FOOD
RESTAURANT ET COMESTIBLES

417. Where is there a good restaurant?
Où peut-on trouver un bon restaurant ?
oo puh-tawn troo-vay uhn bawn rehs-taw-rahn ?

418. Breakfast.   Lunch.   Dinner.
Le petit déjeuner.   Le déjeuner.   Le
dîner.
luh puh-tee day-zhuh-nay.   luh day-zhuh-nay.
luh dee-nay.

419. Supper.   A sandwich.   A snack.
Le souper.   Un sandwich.   Un goûter.
luh soo-pay.   uhn sahn-weetch.   uhn goo-tay.

420. At what time is dinner served?
À quelle heure servez-vous le dîner?
ah keh luhr sehr-vay-voo luh dee-nay?

421. Can we lunch (dine) now?
Pouvons-nous déjeuner (dîner) maintenant?
*poo-vawn-noo day-zhuh-nay (dee-nay) ment-
nahn?*

**422. The waitress.   The waiter.   The head-
waiter.**
La serveuse.   Le garçon.   Le maître
d'hôtel.
*la sehr-vuhz.   luh gar-sawn.   luh MEH-truh
doh-tehl.*

423. Waiter!
Garçon!
gar-sawn!

424. There are two (five) of us.
Nous sommes deux (cinq).
noo sawm duh (senk).

425. Give me a table near the window.
Donnez-moi une table près de la fenêtre.
*daw-nay-mwah ewn TA-bluh preh duh la fuh-
NEH-truh.*

426. At the side.   In the corner.
Sur le côté.   De coin.
sewr luh koh-tay.   duh kwen.

427. Is this table reserved?
Est-ce que cette table est réservée?
ehs kuh seht TA-bluh eh ray-zehr-vay?

428. That one will be free soon.
Celle-là sera libre bientôt.
sehl-la suh-ra LEE-bruh byen-toh.

429. We want to dine à la carte.
Nous voulons dîner à la carte.
noo voo-lawn dee-nay ah la kart.

430. Please serve us quickly.
Servez-nous vite, s'il vous plaît.
sehr ·vay noo veet, seel voo pleh.

431. Bring me the menu (wine list).
Apportez-moi le menu (la carte des vins).
ap-pawr-tay-mwah luh muh-new (la kart day ven).

432. I want something simple. Not too spicy.
Je veux quelque chose de simple.   Pas trop épicé.
zhuh vuh kehl-kuh shohz duh SĒN-pluh.   pah troh pay-pee-say.

433. A plate. A knife.
Une assiette.   Un couteau.
ewn a-syeht.   uhn koo-toh.

434. A fork. A large spoon.
Une fourchette.   Une cuiller à soupe.
ewn foor-sheht.   ewn kwee-yeh ra soop.

435. A teaspoon. The bread.
Une cuiller à café.   Le pain.
ewn kwee-yeh ra-ka-fay.   luh pen.

436. The butter.   The cream.
Le beurre.   La crème.
luh buhr.   la krehm.

437. The sugar.   The salt.   The pepper.
Le sucre.   Le sel.   Le poivre.
luh SEW-kruh.   luh sehl.   luh PWAH-vruh.

438. The sauce.   The oil.   The vinegar.
La sauce.   L'huile.   Le vinaigre.
la sohs.   lweel.   luh vee-NEH-gruh.

439. This is not clean.
Ce n'est pas propre.
suh neh pah PRAW-pruh.

440. (A little) more of this.
(Un peu) plus de ceci.
(uhn puh) plus duh suh-see.

441. I have had enough, thanks.
Cela me suffit, merci.
suh-la muh sew-fee, mehr-see.

442. I like the meat rare (well done).
J'aime la viande saignante (bien cuite).
zhehm la vee-ahnd sehn-yahnt (byen kweet).

**443. This is overcooked.   This is under-
cooked.**
C'est trop cuit.   Ce n'est pas assez cuit.
seh troh kwee.   suh neh pah za-say kwee.

444. This is too tough (sweet, sour).
C'est trop dur (sucré, amer).
seh troh dewr (sew-kray, ah-mehr).

445. This is cold.
C'est froid.
seh frwah.

446. Take it away, please.
Emportez-le, s'il vous plaît.
ahn-pawr-tay-luh, seel voo pleh.

447. I did not order this.
Je n'ai pas commandé cela.
zhuh nay pah kaw-mahn-day suh-la.

448. May I change this for —— ?
Pouvez-vous remplacer cela par —— ?
poo-vay-voo rahn-pla-say suh-la par ——?

449. Ask the head-waiter to come here.
Faites venir le maître d'hôtel.
feht vuh-neer luh MEH-truh doh-tehl.

450. The check please.
L'addition, s'il vous plaît.
la-dee-syawn, seel voo pleh.

451. Kindly pay at the cashier's.
Veuillez payer à la caisse.
vuh-yay peh-yay ah la kehss.

452. Is the tip included?
Le pourboire, est-il compris?
luh poor-bwahr, eh-teel kawn-pree?

453. Is the service charge included?
Le service, est-il compris?
luh sehr-vees, eh-teel kawn-pree?

454. Keep the change.
Gardez la monnaie.
gar-day la maw-nay.

455. There is a mistake in the bill.
Il y a une erreur dans l'addition.
eel ya ewn ehr-ruhr dahn la-dee-syawn.

456. What are these charges for?
Pourquoi ces suppléments?
poor-kwah say sew-play-mahn?

CAFE
CAFÉ

460. Bartender.   A cocktail.
Le barman.   Un cocktail.
luh bar-mahn.   uhn kawk-tehl.

461. A drink.
Une boisson.
ewn bwah-sawn.

462. A fruit drink.   A soft drink.
Un jus de fruit.   Une boisson gazeuse.
uhn zhews duh frwee.   ewn bwah-sawn ga-zuhz.

463. A small (large) bottle of ——.
Une petite (grande) bouteille de ——.
ewn puh-teet (grahnd) boo-tay duh ——.

464. A liqueur.
Une liqueur.
ewn lee-kuhr.

465. A glass of —— .
Un verre de —— .
uhn vehr duh —— .

466. Beer (light, dark).
La bière (blonde, brune).
la byehr (blawnd, brewn).

467. Wine (red, white).
Le vin (rouge, blanc).
luh ven (roozh, blahn).

468. Whiskey (and soda).
Le whiskey (avec du soda).
luh wees-kee (a-vehk dew saw-da).

469. Cognac.   Champagne.
Cognac.   Le champagne.
koh-nyak.   luh shahn-PAN-yuh.

470. Let's have another.
Prenons-en un autre.
pruh-nawn zahn nuh NOH-truh.

MENU
MENU

   This section has been alphabetized in French to facilitate the tourist's reading of French menus.

FIRST COURSE

473. Soupe (au poulet, aux légumes).
soop (oh poo-leh, oh lay-gewm).
Soup (chicken, vegetable).

474. Œufs (brouillés, sur le plat).
uh (broo-yay, sewr luh pla).
Eggs (scrambled, fried).

475. Œufs (à la coque, durs).
uh (ah la kawk, dewr).
Eggs (soft-boiled, hard-boiled).

476. Omelette.
awm-leht.
Omelette.

ENTRÉE: MEATS AND FISH
ENTRÉE: VIANDES ET POISSONS

477. Bœuf. *buhf.* **Beef.**

478. Canard. *ka-nar.* **Duck.**

479. Crevettes. *kruh-veht.* **Shrimp.**

480. Foie. *fwah.* **Liver.**

481. Gigot. *zhee-goh.* **Lamb.**

482. Homard. *aw-mar.* **Lobster.**

483. Oie. *wah.* **Goose.**

484. Porc. *pawr.* **Pork.**

485. Poulet (rôti, frit).
poo-leh (roh-tee, free).
Chicken (roast, fried).

486. Rosbif. *raws-beef.* **Roast beef.**

487. Sardines. *sar-deen.* **Sardines.**

488. Saucisse. *saw-sees.* **Sausage.**

489. Saucisson.   *saw-see-sawn*.   **Salami.**

490. Saumon.   *saw-mawn*.   **Salmon.**

491. Steak.   *stehk*.   **Steak.**

492. Une tranche de ——.

ewn *trahnsh duh* ——.

A slice of ——.

493. Veau.   *voh*.   **Veal.**

VEGETABLES AND SALAD
LÉGUMES ET SALADE

496. Asperges.   *as-pehrzh*.   **Asparagus.**

497. Ail.   *AH-yuh*.   **Garlic.**

498. Carottes.   *ka-rawt*.   **Carrots.**

499. Champignons.   *shahn-peen-yawn*.   **Mush-rooms.**

500. Chou.   *shoo*.   **Cabbage.**

501. Choucroute.   *shoo-kroot*.   **Sauerkraut.**

502. Chou-fleur.   *shoo-fluhr*.   **Cauliflower.**

503. Concombre.   *kawn-KAWN-bruh*.   **Cucumber.**

504. Épinards.   *ay-pee-nahr*.   **Spinach.**

505. Haricots.   *ah-ree-koh*.   **Beans.**

506. Laitue.   *leh-tew*.   **Lettuce.**

507. Mais.   *ma-ees*.   **Corn.**

508. Oignon.   *awn-yawn*.   **Onion.**

509. Petits pois.　*puh-tee pwah.*　**Peas.**

510. Poivres.　*PWAHV-ruh.*　**Peppers.**

511. Pommes de terre (frites, bouillies).
pawm duh tehr (freet, boo-yee).
Potatoes (fried, boiled).

512. Purée de pommes de terre.
pew-ray duh pawm duh tehr.
Mashed potatoes.

513. Tomates.　*taw-mat.*　**Tomatoes.**

FRUITS
FRUITS

516. Cacahuètes.　*ka-ka-weht.*　**Peanuts.**

517. Cerises.　*suh-reez.*　**Cherries.**

518. Citron.　*see-trawn.*　**Lemon.**

519. Fraises.　*frehz.*　**Strawberries.**

520. Framboises.　*frahn-bwahz.*　**Raspberries.**

521. Melon.　*muh-lawn.*　**Melon.**

522. Noix.　*nwah.*　**Nuts (walnuts).**

523. Olives (noires, vertes).
aw-leev (nwahr, vehrt).
Olives (black, green).

524. Orange.　*aw-rahnzh.*　**Orange.**

525. Pamplemousse.　*pahn-pluh-moos.*　**Grape-fruit.**

526. Pastèque.　*pas-tehk.*　**Watermelon.**

527. Pêche. *pehsh.* **Peach.**

528. Pomme. *pawm.* **Apple.**

529. Purée de pommes.
pew-ray duh pawm.
Apple sauce.

530. Raisins. *ray-zen.* **Grapes.**

531. Raisins de Corinthe.
ray-zen duh kaw-rent.
Raisins.

BEVERAGES
BOISSONS

534. Café (noir, avec crème).
ka-fay (nwahr, a-vehk krehm).
Coffee (black, with cream).

535. Citronnade. *see-traw-nad.* **Lemonade.**

536. Lait. *leh.* **Milk.**

537. Thé. *tay.* **Tea.**

DESSERTS
DESSERTS

538. Chocolat. *shaw-kaw-la.* **Chocolate.**

539. Confiture. *kawn-fee-tewr.* **Jam.**

540. Crème. *krehm.* **Custard.**

541. Gâteau. *gah-toh.* **Cake.**

542. Glace. *glas.* **Ice-cream.**

543. Petits gâteaux secs.
puh-tee gah-toh sehk.
Cookies.

544. Vanille. *va-NEE-yuh.* **Vanilla.**

OTHER FOODS
AUTRES NOURRITURES

546. Fromage. *fraw-mazh.* **Cheese.**

547. Gruau. *grew-oh.* **Oatmeal.**

548. Moutarde. *moo-tard.* **Mustard.**

549. Nouilles. *NOO-yuh.* **Noodles.**

550. Pain grillé. *pen gree-yay.* **Toast.**

551. Riz. *ree.* **Rice.**

CHURCH
ÉGLISE

554. A Catholic church.
Une église catholique.
ewn ay-gleez ka-taw-leek.

555. A Protestant (Anglican) church.
Un temple protestant (anglican).
uhn TAHN-pluh praw-tehs-tahn (ahn-glee-kahn).

556. A synagogue.
Une synagogue.
ewn see-na-gawg.

557. Where is there a service in English?
Où y a-t-il un office en anglais?
oo ya tee luh naw-fees ah nahn-gleh?

558. When is the service (mass)?

Quand est l'office (la messe)?

kahn teh law-fees (la mehss)?

559. Is there an English-speaking priest (rabbi, minister)?

Y a-t-il un prêtre (rabbin, ministre) qui parle anglais?

ya tee luhn PREH-truh (ra-ben, mee-NEES-truh) kee par lahn-gleh?

SIGHTSEEING
TOURISME

562. I want a guide who speaks English.

Je désire un guide qui parle anglais.

zhuh day-zeer uhn gheed kee par lahn-gleh.

563. What is the charge per hour (day)?

Quel est le prix par heure (jour)?

keh leh luh pree par ruhr (zhoor)?

564. I am interested in archeology.

Je m'intéresse à l'archéologie.

zhuh men-tay-rehs ah lar-kay-aw-law-zhee.

565. Native arts and crafts.

L'artisanat.

lar-tee-za-na.

566. Painting. Sculpture. Ruins.

La peinture. La sculpture. Les ruines.

la pen-tewr. la skewl-tewr. lay rew-een.

567. Shall I have time to visit the museums?

Est-ce que j'aurai le temps de visiter les musées?

ehss kuh zhaw-ray luh t̄ahn duh vee-zee-tay lay mew-zay?

568. The cathedral.   The monastery.

La cathédrale.   Le monastère.

la ka-tay-dral.   luh maw-nas-tehr.

569. The castle.

Le château.

luh shah-toh.

570. Is it (still) open?

Est-ce (encore) ouvert?

ehss (āhn-kawr) oo-vehr?

571. How long does it stay open?

Combien de temps reste-t-on ouvert?

kawn-byen duh t̄ahn rehst taw   noo-vehr?

572. How long must I wait?

Combien de temps dois-je attendre?

kawn-byen duh t̄ahn dwah zha-T̄AHN-druh?

573. Where is the entrance (exit)?

Où est l'entrée (la sortie)?

oo eh l̄ahn-tray (la sawr-tee)?

574. What is the price of admission?

Quel est le prix d'entrée?

keh leh luh pree d̄ahn-tray?

575. Do we need a guide?
Faut-il un guide?
foh tee luhn gheed?

576. How much is the guidebook?
Quel est le prix d'un guide?
keh leh luh pree duhn gheed?

577. May I take photographs?
Est-il permis de prendre des photos?
eh teel pehr-mee duh PRAHN-druh day faw-toh?

578. Do you sell postcards?
Vendez-vous des cartes postales?
vahn-day-voo day kart paws-tal?

**579. Do you have a book in English about
——?**
Avez-vous un livre en anglais sur ——?
ah-vay-voo zuhn LEE-vrah nahn-gleh sewr ——?

580. Take me back to the hotel.
Ramenez-moi à l'hôtel.
ram-nay mwah ah loh-tehl.

581. Go back by way of ——.
Rentrez par ——.
rahn-tray par ——.

AMUSEMENTS
AMUSEMENTS

584. A concert. Movies. Folk dances.
Un concert. Le cinéma. Des danses de
folklore.
*uhn kawn-sehr. luh see-nay-ma. day dahns
duh fawk-lawr.*

585. The beach.　Tennis.　Golf.　Horse-racing.

La plage.　Le tennis.　Le golf.　Les courses.

la plazh.　luh teh-nees.　luh gawlf.　lay koorss.

586. Skiing.　Skating.　Soccer.

Le ski.　Le patinage.　Le football.

luh skee.　luh pa-tee-nazh.　luh foot-bal.

587. Night club.　The opera.　The theatre.

La boîte de nuit.　L'opéra.　Le théâtre.

la bwaht duh nwee.　loh-pay-ra.　luh tay-AH-truh.

588. Is there a matinee today?

Y a-t-il matinée aujourd'hui?

ya teel ma-tee-nay oh-zhoord-wee?

589. When does the evening performance (floorshow) start?

À quelle heure commence la soirée (le spectacle)?

ah keh luhr kaw-mahns la swah-ray (luh spehk-TA-kluh)?

590. Cover charge.　Minimum.

Le couvert.　Le minimum.

luh koo-vehr.　luh mee-nee-muhm.

591. Where can we go to dance?

Où pouvons-nous aller danser?

oo poo-vawn-noo zal-lay dahn-say?

592. Have you any seats for tonight?
Avez-vous des places pour ce soir?
ah-vay-voo day plass poor suh swahr?

593. An orchestra seat.   A reserved seat.
Un fauteuil d'orchestre.   Une place réservée.
uhn foh-TUH-yuh dawr-KEHS-truh.   ewn plas ray-zehr-vay.

594. In the balcony.   The box.
Au balcon.   La loge.
oh bal-kawn.   la lawzh.

595. Newsreel.   Box office.
Les actualités.   Le bureau de location.
lay zak-tew-ah-lee-tay.   luh bew-roh duh law-ka-syawn.

596. Can I see (hear) well from there?
Pourrai-je voir (entendre) bien de là?
poo-RAY-zhuh vwahr (ahn-TAHN-druh) byen duh la?

597. Not too near (far).
Pas trop près (loin).
pah troh preh (lwen).

598. The music is excellent.
La musique est excellente.
la mew-zeek eh tehk-sehl-lahnt.

599. This is very interesting (funny).
C'est très intéressant (amusant).
seh treh zen-tay-rehs-sahn (za-mew-zahn).

600. May I have this dance?

Voulez-vous danser?

voo-lay-voo dahn-say?

601. Is this the intermission?

Est-ce maintenant l'entr'acte?

ehss ment-nahn lahn-trakt?

SHOPPING AND PERSONAL SERVICES
ACHATS ET SERVICES

604. I want to go shopping.

Je veux courir les magasins.

zhuh vuh koo-reer lay ma-ga-zen.

605. Where is the bakery (pastry shop)?

Où est la boulangerie (la pâtisserie)?

oo eh la boo-lahnzh-ree (la pah-teess-ree)?

606. A candy store.   A cigar store.

Une confiserie.   Un bureau de tabac.

ewn kawn-feez-ree.   uhn bew-roh duh ta-bah.

607. A clothing store.   A department store.

Une maison de vêtements.   Un grand magasin.

ewn meh-zawn duh veht-mahn.   uhn grahn ma-ga-zen.

608. A drug store.   A grocery.

Une pharmacie.   Une épicerie.

ewn far-ma-see.   ewn ay-peess-ree.

609. A hardware store.   A hat shop.

Une quincaillerie.   Une chapellerie.

ewn ken·kah·yuh-ree.   ewn sha-pehl-ree.

610. A jewelry store.   A shoe store.
Une bijouterie.   Une maison de chaussures.
*ewn bee-zhoot-ree.   ewn meh-zawn duh shoh-
sewr.*

611. A meat market.   A tailor shop.
Une boucherie.   Chez le tailleur.
ewn boosh-ree.   shay luh ta-yuhr.

612. Shoemaker.   Watchmaker.
Le cordonnier.   L'horloger.
luh kawr-daw-nyay.   lawr-law-zhay.

See also CLOTHING, COMMON OBJECTS, page 77, 105.

615. Sale.   Bargain sale.
Vente.   Réclame *or* Solde.
vahnt.   ray-klam OR *sawld.*

616. I want to buy ——.
Je veux acheter ——.
zhuh vuh zash-tay ——.

617. I (I do not) like that.
J'aime (je n'aime pas) cela.
zhehm (zhuh nehm pah) suh-la.

618. How much is it?
Combien est-ce?
kawn-byen ehss?

619. It is very (too) expensive.
C'est très (trop) cher.
seh treh (troh) shehr.

620. I prefer something better (cheaper).

Je préfère quelque chose de mieux (de moins cher).

zhuh pray-fehr kehl-kuh-shohz duh myuh (duh mwen shehr).

621. Show me some others.

Montrez-m'en d'autres.

mawn-tray-mahn DOH-truh.

622. May I try this on?

Puis-je l'essayer?

PWEE-zhuh leh-say-yay?

623. Can I order one?

Puis-je en commander un?

PWEE-zhahn kaw-mahn-day uhn?

624. How long will it take?

Combien de temps dois-je attendre?

kawn-byen duh tahn dwah zhah-TAHN-druh?

625. Please take my measurements.

Veuillez prendre mes mesures.

vuh-yay PRAHN-druh may muh-zewr.

See also MEASUREMENTS, page 103.

626. It does not fit me.

Il ne me va pas.

eel nuh muh va pah.

627. It is too long (short).

C'est trop long (court).

seh troh lawn (koor).

628. It is (not) becoming to me.
Il (ne) me va (pas).
eel (nuh) muh va (pah).

629. Will you wrap this please?
Voulez-vous bien l'envelopper?
voo-lay-voo byen lahn-vuh-law-pay?

630. Can you ship it to ——?
Pouvez-vous l'expédier à ——?
poo-vay-voo lehx-pay-dyay ah ——?

631. Whom do I pay?
À qui dois-je payer?
ah kee DWAH-zhuh peh-yay?

632. Please bill me.
Veuillez m'envoyer la facture.
vuh-yay mahn-vwah-yay la fak-tewr.

POST OFFICE
LA POSTE

635. Where is the post office?
Où est la poste?
oo eh la pawst?

636. A postcard (letter) to ——.
Une carte postale (lettre) à ——.
ewn kart paws-tal (LEH-truh) a ——.

637. How many stamps do I need?
De combien dois-je l'affranchir?
duh kawn-byen DWAH-zhuh laf-rahn-sheer?

638. Three stamps of 50 francs denomination.

Trois timbres de cinquante francs.

trwah TEN-bruh duh sen-kahnt frahn.

639. There is nothing dutiable on this.

Il n'y a rien à déclarer ici.

eel nee ah ree-en ah day-kla-ray ee-see.

640. Will this go out today?

Est-ce que cela partira aujourd'hui ?

ehs-kuh suh-la par-tee-ra oh-zhoor-dwee?

641. Give me a receipt, please.

Donnez-moi un récépissé, s'il vous plaît.

daw-nay-mwah uhn ray-say-pees-say, seel voo pleh.

642. I want to send a money order.

Je veux envoyer un mandat-poste.

zhuh vuh zahn-vwah-yay uhn mahn-da-pawst.

643. To which window do I go?

À quel guichet dois-je m'adresser ?

a kehl ghee-sheh DWAH-zhuh ma-drehs-say?

644. By airmail.   Parcel post.

Par avion.   Le colis postal.

pa rah-vyawn.   luh kaw-lee paws-tal.

645. Registered. Special Delivery. Insured.

Recommandé.   Exprès.   Valeur déclarée.

ruh-kaw-mahn-day.   ehx-preh.   va-luhr day-kla-ray.

BANK
BANQUE

648. Where is the nearest bank?

Où est la banque la plus proche?

oo eh la ba͞hnk la plew prawsh?

649. At which window can I cash this?

À quel guichet puis-je toucher ceci?

ah kehl ghee-sheh PWEE-zhuh too-shay suh-see?

650. Can you change this for me?

Pouvez-vous me le changer?

poo-vay-voo muh luh shahn-zhay?

651. Will you cash a check?

Voulez-vous payer un chèque?

voo-lay-voo pey-yay u͞hn shehk?

652. Give me (do not give me) large bills.

Donnez-moi (ne me donnez pas) de gros billets.

daw-nay-mwah (nuh muh daw-nay pah) duh groh bee-yeh.

653. May I have some change?

Puis-je avoir de la petite monnaie?

PWEE-zha-vwahr duh la puh-teet maw-neh?

654. I have traveler's checks.

J'ai des chèques de voyageur.

zhay day shehk duh vwah-ya-zhuhr.

655. Letter of credit.

Une lettre de crédit.

ewn LEH-truh duh kray-dee.

656. A bank draft.

Une lettre de change.

ewn LEH-truh duh shahnzh.

657. What is the exchange rate on the dollar?

Quel est le cours du change?

keh leh luh koor dew shahnzh?

BOOKSTORE AND STATIONER'S
LIBRAIRIE ET PAPETERIE

660. Where is there a bookstore?

Où se trouve une librairie?

oo suh troov ewn lee-bray-ree?

661. A stationer's.   A news dealer.

Une papeterie. Un marchand de journaux.

ewn pap-tree.   uhn mar-shahn duh zhoor-noh.

662. Newspapers. Magazines. Weeklies.

Les journaux. Les revues. Les hébdomadaires.

lay zhoor-noh. lay ruh-vew. lay zehb-daw-ma-dayr.

663. A dictionary.   A guide book.

Un dictionnaire.   Un guide.

uhn deek-syaw-nayr.   uhn gheed.

664. A map of ——.

Une carte de ——.

ewn kart duh ——.

665. Postcards. Playing cards.
Les cartes postales. Les cartes à jouer.
lay kart paws-tal. lay kart ah zhoo-ay.

666. Greeting cards.
Les cartes de meilleurs vœux.
lay kart duh may-yuhr vuh.

667. Writing paper. Ink. Blotter.
Le papier à lettre. L'encre. Un buvard.
*luh pap-yay ah LEH-truh. LAHN-kruh. uhn
bew-var.*

668. Envelopes (airmail). A pencil.
Les enveloppes (par avion). Un crayon.
*lay zahn-vuh-lawp (pa ra-vyawn). uhn kreh-
yawn.*

669. A fountain pen. Artist's materials.
Un stylo. Des accessoires d'artiste.
uhn stee-loh. day zak-sehs-swahr dar-teest.

670. Cord. String. An eraser.
La corde. La ficelle. Une gomme.
la kawrd. la fee-sehl. ewn gawm.

671. Typewriter ribbon. Carbon paper.
Un ruban pour machine à écrire. Le
papier carbone.
*uhn rew-bahn poor ma-sheen ah ay-kreer.
luh pap-yay kar-bawn.*

672. Tissue paper. Wrapping paper.
Le papier de soie. Le papier d'emballage.
*luh pap-yay duh swah. luh pap-yay dahn-ba-
lazh.*

CIGAR STORE
BUREAU DE TABAC

675. Where is the nearest cigar store?

Où est le bureau de tabac le plus proche?

oo eh luh bew-roh duh ta-bah luh plew prawsh?

676. I want some cigars.

Je veux des cigares.

zhuh vuh day see-gar.

677. A pack of (American) cigarettes, please.

Un paquet de cigarettes (américaines), s'il vous plaît.

uhn pa-keh duh see-ga-reht (za-may-ree-kehn), seel voo pleh.

678. Please show me some cigarette cases.

Veuillez me montrer des étuis à cigarettes.

vuh-yay muh mawn-tray day zay-twee ah see-ga-reht.

679. I need a lighter.

Il me faut un briquet.

eel muh foh uhn bree-keh.

680. Flint. Fluid.

Une pierre. De l'essence.

ewn pee-ehr. duh lehs-sahns.

681. Matches. A pipe.

Des allumettes. Une pipe.

day zal-lew-meht. ewn peep.

682. Pipe tobacco. A pouch.

Du tabac pour la pipe. Une blague à
tabac.

dew ta-ba poor la peep. ewn blag ah ta-ba.

BARBER SHOP AND BEAUTY PARLOR
COIFFEUR ET SALON DE BEAUTÉ

685. Where is there a good barber?

Où se trouve un bon coiffeur?

oo suh troov uhn bawn kwah-fuhr?

686. I want a (haircut, shave).

Je veux me faire (couper les cheveux,
raser).

*zuh vuh muh fehr (koo-pay lay shuh-vuh, ra-
zay).*

687. Not too short.

Pas trop court.

pah troh koor.

688. Do not cut any off the top.

N'en coupez pas sur le dessus.

nahn koo-pay pah sewr luh duh-sew.

689. (Do not) put on oil.

(Pas de) pommade.

(pah duh) paw-mad.

690. I part my hair on the (the other) side.

Je fais ma raie sur le (l'autre) côté.

*zhuh feh ma ray sewr luh (LOH-truh) koh-
tay.*

691. In the middle.

Au milieu.

oh mee-lyuh.

692. The water is too hot (cold).

L'eau est trop chaude (froide).

loh eh troh shohd (frwahd).

693. I want my shoes shined.

Je veux faire cirer mes chaussures.

zhuh vuh fehr see-ray may shoh-sewr.

694. Can I make an appointment for——?

Puis-je prendre rendez-vous pour ——?

PWEE-zhuh PRAHN-druh rahn-day-voo poor ——?

695. I want a shampoo.

Je veux un shampooing.

zhuh vuh zuhn shahn-pwen.

696. A finger wave. A permanent.

Une mise en plis. Une permanente.

ewn meez ahn plee. ewn pehr-ma-nahnt.

697. A facial. A manicure.

Un massage facial. Une manucure.

uhn ma-sazh fa-syal. ewn ma-new-kewr.

PHOTOGRAPHY
PHOTOGRAPHIE

700. I want a roll of (color) film.

Je désire un rouleau de film (en couleur).

zhuh day-zeer uhn roo-loh duh feelm (ahn koo-luhr).

701. The size is ——.
Numéro ——.
new-may-roh ——.

702. Movie film.   For this camera.
Du film cinékodak.   Pour cet appareil.
dew feelm see-nay-kaiv-dak.   poor seh ta-pa-ray.

703. What is the charge for developing a roll?
Combien prenez-vous pour développer une bobine?
kawn-byen pruh-nay-voo poor dayv-law-pay ewn baw-been?

704. For one print of each.
Pour une épreuve de chaque.
poor ew nay-pruhv duh shak.

705. For an enlargement.
Pour un agrandissement.
poo ruh na-grahn-deess-mahn.

706. When will they be ready?
Quand seront-ils prêts?
kahn suh-rawn-teel preh?

707. The camera is out of order.
L'appareil est déréglé.
la pa-ray eh day-ray-glay.

708. Do you rent cameras?
Louez-vous des appareils?
loo-ay-voo day za-pa-ray?

709. I should like one for today.

J'en voudrais un pour aujourd'hui.

zhahn voo-dreh zuhn poo raw-zhoor-dwee.

LAUNDRY AND DRY CLEANING
BLANCHISSERIE ET TEINTURERIE

712. Where is the nearest laundry (dry cleaner)?

Où est la blanchisserie (teinturerie) la plus proche?

oo eh la blahn-sheess-ree (ten-tewr-ree) la plew prawsh?

713. To be washed (mended).

À faire laver (repriser).

ah fehr la-vay (ruh-pree-zay).

714. To be cleaned (pressed).

À faire nettoyer (repasser).

ah fehr neh-twah-yay (ruh-pa-say).

715. Do not wash this in hot water.

Ne lavez pas ceci dans de l'eau chaude.

nuh la-vay pah suh-see dahn duh loh shohd.

716. Use lukewarm water.

Prenez de l'eau tiède.

pruh-nay duh loh tee-ehd.

717. Be very careful.

Faites bien attention.

feht byen ah-tahn-syawn.

718. Do not dry this in the sun.
Ne le faites pas sécher au soleil.
nuh luh feht pah say-shay oh saw-lay.

719. (Do not) starch the collars.
Veuillez (ne pas) amidonner les cols.
vuh-yay (nuh pah) ah-mee-daw-nay lay kawl.

720. When can I have this?
Quand pouvez-vous me rendre ceci?
kahn poo-vay-voo muh RAHN-druh suh-see?

721. The belt is missing.
La ceinture manque.
la sen-tewr mahnk.

CLOTHING
VÊTEMENTS

724. Apron. Un tablier. *uhn ta-blee-ay.*

725. Bathing cap. Un bonnet de bain.
uhn baw-neh duh ben.

726. Bathing suit. Un costume de bain.
uhn kaws-tewm duh ben.

727. Blouse. Un corsage. *uhn kawr-sazh.*

728. Brassiere. Un soutien-gorge.
uhn soo-tyen-gawrzh.

729. Coat. Un manteau. *uhn mahn-toh.*

730. Collar. Le col. *luh kawl.*

731. Diapers. Les couches. *lay koosh.*

732. Dress. La robe. *la rawb.*

733. Garters.   Les jarretières.   *lay zhar-tyehr.*

734. Gloves.   Les gants.   *lay gahn.*

735. Handkerchief.   Le mouchoir.
luh moo-shwahr.

736. Hat.   Le chapeau.   *luh sha-poh.*

737. Jacket.   La jaquette.   *la zha-keht.*

738. Necktie.   La cravate.   *la kra-vat.*

739. Nightgown.   La chemise de nuit.
la shuh-meez duh nwee.

740. Overcoat.   Le pardessus.
luh par-duh-sew.

741. Pajamas.   Le pyjama.
luh pee-zha-ma.

742. Panties.   La culotte.   *la kew-lawt.*

743. Petticoat.   Le jupon.   *luh zhew-pawn.*

744. Raincoat.   L'imperméable.
len-pehr-may-AH-bluh.

745. Robe.   La robe de chambre.
la rawb duh SHAHN-bruh.

746. Scarf.   L'écharpe.   *lay-sharp.*

747. Shirt.   La chemise.   *la shuh-meez.*

748. Shorts.   Le caleçon.   *luh kal-sawn.*

749. Skirt.   La jupe.   *la zhewp.*

750. Slip.   La combinaison.
la kawn-bee-neh-zawn.

751. Shoes.   Les chaussures.   *lay shoh-sewr.*

752. Slippers.   Les pantoufles.
lay pahn-TOO-fluh.

753. Socks.   Les chaussettes.   *lay shoh-seht.*

754. (Nylon) stockings.   Les bas (de nylon).
lay bah (duh nee-lawn).

755. Suit.   Le costume.   *luh kaws-tewm.*

756. Suspenders.   Les bretelles.
lay bruh-tehl.

757. Sweater.   Le sweater.   *luh sweh-tayr.*

758. Trousers.   Le pantalon.
luh pahn-ta-lawn.

759. Undershirt.   Le tricot.   *luh tree-koh.*

760. Underwear.   Les sous-vêtements.
lay soo-veht-mahn.

761. Vest.   Le gilet.   *luh gee-leh.*

HEALTH AND ACCIDENTS
SANTÉ ET ACCIDENTS

765. There has been an accident.
Il y a eu un accident.
eel ya ew uh nak-see-dahn.

766. Get a doctor (nurse).
Faites venir un médecin (une infirmière).
feht vuh-neer uhn mayd-sen (ewn en-feer-myehr).

767. Send for an ambulance.
Envoyer chercher une ambulance.
ahn-vwah-yay shehr-shay ewn ahn-bew-lahns.

768. Please bring blankets.

Veuillez apporter des couvertures.

vuh-yay za-pawr-tay day koo-vehr-tewr.

769. A stretcher.   Water.

Un brancard.   De l'eau.

uhn brahn-kar.   duh loh.

770. He is (seriously) injured.

Il est (gravement) blessé.

eel eh (grav-mahn) bleh-say.

771. Help me carry him.

Aidez-moi à le porter.

eh-day-mwah ah luh pawr-tay.

772. He was knocked down.

On l'a renversé.

awn la rahn-vehr-say.

773. She has fallen (has fainted).

Elle est tombée (s'est évanouie).

ehl eh tawn-bay (seh tay-va-noo-ee).

774. I feel weak.

Je me sens faible.

zhuh muh sahn FEH-bluh.

775. He has a fracture (bruise, cut).

Il a une fracture (blessure, coupure).

eel ah ewn frak-tewr (bleh-sewr, koo-pewr).

776. He has burned (cut) his hand.

Il s'est brûlé (coupé) la main.

eel seh brew-lay (koo-pay) la men.

777. It is bleeding.
Ça saigne.
sa SEHN-yuh.

778. It is swollen.
C'est enflé.
seh tahn-flay.

779. Can you dress this?
Pouvez-vous le panser?
poo-vay-voo luh pahn-say?

780. Have you any bandages (splints)?
Avez-vous des pansements (des éclisses)?
ah-vay-voo day pahns-mahn (day zay-klees)?

781. I need something for a tourniquet.
Il me faut quelque chose pour un tourniquet.
*eel muh foh KEHL-kuh shohz poo ruhn toor-
nee-keh.*

782. Are you all right?
Êtes-vous bien?
eht-voo byen?

783. It hurts here.
J'ai des douleurs ici.
zhay day doo-luhr zee-see.

784. I want to sit down a moment.
Je veux m'asseoir un moment.
zhuh vuh ma-swah ruhn maw-mahn.

785. I cannot move my ——.
Je ne peux pas bouger mon ——.
zhuh nuh puh pah boo-zhay mawn ——.

786. I have hurt my ——.

Je me suis fait mal à ——.

zhuh muh swee feh mal ah ——.

See PARTS OF THE BODY, page 91.

789. Can I travel on Monday?

Est-ce que je pourrai voyager lundi?

ehs-kuh zhuh poor-ray vwah-ya-zhay luhn-dee?

790. Please notify my husband (wife).

Veuillez prévenir mon mari (ma femme).

vuh-yay prayv-neer mawn ma-ree (ma fahm).

791. Here is my identification (my card).

Voici mon identification (ma carte).

vwah-see maw nee-dahn-tee-fee-ka-syawn (ma kart).

ILLNESS
MALADIE

794. I wish to see a doctor (specialist).

Je veux voir un médecin (un spécialiste).

zhuh vuh vwah ruhn mayd-sen (uhn spay-sya-leest).

795. An American doctor.

Un médecin américain.

uhn mayd-sen na-may-ree-ken.

796. I do not sleep well.

Je ne dors pas bien.

zhuh nuh dawr pah byen.

797. My foot hurts.

J'ai mal au pied.

zhay mal oh pyay.

798. My head aches.
J'ai mal à la tête.
zhay mal ah la teht.

799. I have an abscess.
J'ai un abcès.
zhay uh nab-seh.

800. Appendicitis.   Biliousness.
L'appendicite.   La bile.
la-pahn-dee-seet.   la beel.

801. A bite.   An insect bite.   A blister.
Une morsure.   Une piqûre.   Une ampoule.
ewn mawr-sewr.   ewn pee-kewr.   ewn ahn-
pool.

802. A boil.   A burn.
Un furoncle.   Une brûlure.
uhn few-RAWN-kluh.   ewn brew-lewr.

803. Chills.   A cold.
Un refroidissement.   Un rhume.
uhn ruh-frwah-deess-mahn.   uhn rewm.

804. Constipation.   A cough.
La constipation.   Une toux.
la kawn-stee-pa-syawn.   ewn too.

805. A cramp.   Diarrhoea.
Une crampe.   La diarrhée.
ewn krahnp.   la dee-ah-ray.

806. Dysentery.   An earache.
La dysenterie.   Un mal d'oreille.
la dee-sahn-tree.   uhn mal daw-ray.

807. A fever.   Food poisoning.
Une fièvre.   Un empoisonnement.
ewn FYEH-vruh.   uh nahn-pwah-zawn-mahn.

808. Hoarseness.   Indigestion.
L'enrouement.   L'indigestion.
lahn-roo-mahn.   len-dee-zhehs-tyawn.

809. Nausea.   Pneumonia.
La nausée.   La pneumonie.
la naw-say.   la pnuh-maw-nee.

810. A sore throat.
Un mal de gorge.
uhn mal duh gawrzh.

811. Chafed.   A sprain.
Irrité.   Une entorse.
ee-ree-tay.   ew nahn-tawrs.

812. Sun burn.   Sun stroke.
Un coup de soleil.   L'insolation.
uhn koo duh saw-lay.   len-saw-la-syawn.

813. Typhoid fever.   To vomit.
La fièvre typhoïde.   Vomir.
la FYEH-vruh tee-faw-eed.   vaw-meer.

814. What am I to do?
Que dois-je faire?
kuh DWAH-zhuh fehr?

815. Must I stay in bed?
Dois-je rester au lit?
DWAH-zhuh rehs-tay oh lee?

816. Do I have to go to a hospital?
Dois-je aller à un hôpital?
DWAH-zhuh al-lay ah uh noh-pee-tal?

817. May I get up?
Puis-je me lever?
PWEE-zhuh muh luh-vay?

818. I feel better.
Je me sens mieux.
zhuh muh sahn myuh.

819. When do you think I'll be better?
Quand pensez-vous que je sois remis?
kahn pahn-say-voo kuh zhuh swah ruh-mee?

820. When will you come again?
Quand allez-vous revenir?
kahn tal-lay-voo ruhv-neer?

821. A drop.   A teaspoonful.
Une goutte.   Une cuillerée.
ewn goot.   ewn kwee-yuh-ray.

822. Hot water.   Ice.   Medicine.
De l'eau chaude.   De la glace.   Le médicament.
duh loh shohd.   duh la glas.   luh may-dee-ka-mahn.

823. A pill.   A prescription.
Une pillule.   Une ordonnance.
ewn pee-lewl.   ewn awr-daw-nahns.

824. Every hour.   Before (after) meals.
　　Toutes les heures.   Avant (après) les repas.
　　toot lay zuhr.   a-vahn (a-preh) lay ruh-pah.

825. Twice a day.
　　Deux fois par jour.
　　duh fwah par zhoor.

826. On going to bed.   On getting up.
　　En se couchant.   En se levant.
　　ahn suh koo-shahn.   ahn suh luh-vahn.

827. X-rays.
　　Les rayons-X.
　　lay ra-yawn zeeks.

See also DRUG STORE, page 87.

DENTIST
DENTISTE

830. Do you know a good dentist?
　　Connaissez-vous un bon dentiste?
　　kaw-nehs-say-voo zuhn bawn dahn-teest?

831. This tooth hurts.
　　Cette dent me fait mal.
　　seht dahn muh feh mal.

832. Can you fix it (temporarily)?
　　Pouvez-vous l'arranger (provisoirement)?
　　poo-vay-voo lar-rahn-zhay (praw-vee-zwahr-mahn)?

833. I have lost a filling.
　　J'ai perdu un plombage.
　　zhay pehr-dew uhn plawn-bazh.

834. I have broken a tooth.

Je me suis cassé une dent.

zhuh muh swee kas-say ewn dahn.

835. I (I do not) want it extracted.

Je veux (je ne veux pas) la faire arracher.

zhuh vuh (zhuh nuh vuh pah) la feh rar-ra-shay.

836. Can you save it?

Pouvez-vous la conserver?

poo-vay-voo la kawn-sehr-vay?

837. You are hurting me.

Vous me faites mal.

voo muh feht mal.

838. Can you repair this denture?

Pouvez-vous réparer ce dentier?

poo-vay-voo ray-pa-ray suh dahn-tyay?

839. Local anesthesia.

Une anesthésie locale.

ewn a-nehs-tay-zee law-kal.

840. The gums.   The nerve.

Les gencives.   Le nerf.

lay zhahn-seev.   luh nehr.

DRUG STORE

PHARMACIE

841. Where is there a drug store where they understand English?

Où y a-t-il une pharmacie où l'on comprend l'anglais?

oo ya tee-lewn far-ma-see oo lawn kawn-prahn lahn-gleh?

842. Can you fill this prescription?
Pouvez-vous remplir cette ordonnance?
poo-vay-voo rahn-pleer seht awr-daw-nahns?

843. How long will it take?
Combien de temps vous faudra-t-il?
kawn-byen duh tahn voo foh-dra teel?

844. I want adhesive tape.
Je veux du sparadrap.
zhuh vuh dew spa-ra-drah.

845. Alcohol. L'alcool. *lal-kawl.*

846. Antiseptic. L'antiseptique.
lahn-tee-sehp-teek.

847. Aspirin. L'aspirine. *las-pee-reen.*

848. Analgesic. L'analgésique.
la-nal-zhay-zeek.

849. Bandages. Les pansements.
lay pahnss-mahn.

850. Bicarbonate of soda.
Du bicarbonate de soude.
dew bee-kar-baw-nat duh sood.

851. Boric acid. De l'acide borique.
duh la-seed baw-reek.

852. A (hair, tooth) brush.
Une brosse (à cheveux, à dents).
ewn brawss (a shuh-vuh, a dahn).

853. Carbolic acid. Du phénol.
dew fay-nawl.

854. Castor oil. De l'huile de ricin.
duh lweel duh ree-sen.

855. Cleaning fluid. Le produit détachant.
luh praw-dwee day-ta-shahn.

856. Cold cream. Du cold-cream.
dew "cold cream."

857. A comb. Un peigne. *uhn PEHN-yuh.*

858. Corn pads. Les toiles anticor.
lay twal zahn-tee-kawr.

859. Cotton. De l'ouate. *duh luh-wat.*

860. A depilatory. Un dépilatoire.
uhn day-pee-la-twahr.

861. A deodorant. Un désodorisant.
uhn day-zaw-daw-ree-zahn.

862. Ear stoppers. Les protège-oreilles.
lay praw-TEH-zhaw-REH-yuh.

863. Epsom salts. Des sels d'Epsom.
day sehl dehp-sawm.

864. An eye cup. Une œillère. *ew nuh-yehr.*

865. Gauze. De la gaze. *duh la gaz.*

866. A hot water bottle. Une bouillote.
ewn boo-yawt.

867. An ice bag. Un sac à glace.
uhn sak ah glas.

868. Insect bite lotion.
Lotion contre les piqûres d'insecte.
law-syawn KAWN-truh lay pee-kewr den-sehkt.

869. Insect repellent.   Lotion antimoustique.
law-sawn ahn-tee-mooss-teek.

870. Iodine.   De l'iode.   *duh lee-awd.*

871. A laxative.   Un laxatif.   *uhn lax-ah-teef.*

872. Lipstick.   Du rouge à lèvres.
dew roozh ah LEH-vruh.

873. A medicine dropper.
Un compte-gouttes.
uhn kawnt-goot.

874. A mouthwash.   De l'eau dentifrice.
duh loh dahn-tee-freess.

875. Peroxide.   De l'eau oxygénée.
duh loh awk-see-zhay-nay.

876. Poison.   Du poison.   *dew pwah-zawn.*

877. Powder.   Du talc.   *dew talc.*

878. Quinine.   De la quinine.   *duh la kee-neen.*

879. A razor.   Un rasoir.   *uhn ra-zwahr.*

880. Razor blades.   Des lames de rasoir.
day lam duh ra-zwahr.

881. Rouge.   Du rouge.   *dew roozh.*

882. Sanitary napkins.
Des serviettes hygiéniques.
day sehr-vee-eht zee-zhee-ay-neek.

883. A sedative.   Un calmant.   *uhn kal-mahn.*

884. Shampoo (liquid, cream).
Le shampooing (liquide, crème).
luh shahn-pwen (lee-keed, krehm).

885. Shaving lotion.   Lotion après la barbe.
law-syawn a-preh la barb.

886. Shaving cream (brushless).
La crème à raser (pour sans blaireau).
la krehm ah rah-zay (poor sahn blay-roh).

887. Cake of soap.   La savonnette.
la sa-vaw-neht.

888. Sunburn ointment.   L'huile anti-solaire.
lweel ahn-tee-saw-layr.

889. Smelling salts.   Des sels ammoniaques.
day sehl zam-maw-nee-ak.

890. Suntan oil.   L'huile de soleil.
lweel duh saw-lay.

891. Thermometer.   Le thermomètre.
luh tehr-maw-MEH-truh.

892. Toothpaste.   La pâte dentifrice.
la paht dahn-tee-freess.

893. Toothpowder.   La poudre dentifrice.
la POO-druh dahn-tee-freess.

PARTS OF THE BODY
CORPS

894. The ankle.   La cheville.
la shuh-VEE-yuh.

895. The appendix.   L'appendice.
lap-pahn-deess.

896. The arm.   Le bras.   *luh bra.*

897. The back.   Le dos.   *luh doh.*

898. The blood.   Le sang.   *luh sahn.*

899. The bone.   L'os.   *lawss.*

900. The bones.   Les os.   *lay zoh.*

901. The cheek.   La joue.   *la zhoo.*

902. The chest.   La poitrine.   *la pwah-treen.*

903. The chin.   Le menton.   *luh mahn-tawn.*

904. The collar bone.   La clavicule.   *la kla-vee-kewl.*

905. The ear.   L'oreille.   *law-REH-yuh.*

906. The elbow.   Le coude.   *luh kood.*

907. The eye.   L'œil.   *LUH-yuh.*

908. The eyebrows.   Les sourcils.   *lay soor-see.*

909. The eyelashes.   Les cils.   *lay seel.*

910. The eyelid.   La paupière.   *la poh-pyehr.*

911. The face.   Le visage.   *luh vee-zazh.*

912. The finger.   Le doigt.   *luh dwah.*

913. The foot.   Le pied.   *luh pyay.*

914. The forehead.   Le front.   *luh frawn.*

915. The hair.   Les cheveux.   *lay shuh-vuh.*

916. The hand.   La main.   *la men.*

917. The head.   La tête.   *la teht.*

918. The heart.   Le cœur.   *luh kuhr.*

919. The heel. Le talon. *luh ta-lawn.*

920. The hip. La hanche. *la ahnsh.*

921. The intestines. Les intestins. *lay zen-tehs-ten.*

922. The jaw. La mâchoire. *la mah-shwahr.*

923. The joint. La jointure. *la zhwen-tewr.*

924. The kidney. Le rein. *luh ren.*

925. The knee. Le genou. *luh zhuh-noo.*

926. The leg. La jambe. *la zhahnb.*

927. The lip. La lèvre. *la LEH-vruh.*

928. The liver. Le foie. *luh fwah.*

929. The lung. Le poumon. *luh poo-mawn.*

930. The mouth. La bouche. *la boosh.*

931. The muscle. Le muscle. *luh MEWS-kluh.*

932. The nail. L'ongle. *LAWN-gluh.*

933. The neck. Le cou. *luh koo.*

934. The nerve. Le nerf. *luh nehr.*

935. The nose. Le nez. *luh nay.*

936. The rib. La côte. *la koht.*

937. The shoulder. L'épaule. *lay-pawl.*

938. The right (left) side. Le côté droit (gauche).
luh koh-tay drwah (gohsh).

939. The skin. La peau. *la poh.*

940. The skull.   Le crâne.   *luh krahn.*

941. The spine.   La colonne vertébrale.
la kaw-lawn vehr-tay-bral.

942. The stomach.   Le ventre.   *luh V$\overline{AHN}$-truh.*

943. The tooth.   La dent.   *la da$\overline{hn}$.*

944. The thigh.   La cuisse.   *la kweess.*

945. The throat.   La gorge.   *la gawrzh.*

946. The thumb.   Le pouce.   *luh pooss.*

947. The toe.   L'orteil.   *lawr-tay.*

948. The tongue.   La langue.   *la la$\overline{hng}$.*

949. The tonsils.   Les amygdales.   *lay za-meeg-dal.*

950. The waist.   La taille.   *la TA-yuh.*

951. The wrist.   Le poignet.   *luh pwahn-yeh.*

COMMUNICATIONS: TELEPHONE
COMMUNICATIONS: TÉLÉPHONE

953. Where can I telephone?
Où puis-je téléphoner?
oo PWEE-zhuh tay-lay-faw-nay?

954. Will you telephone for me?
Voulez-vous bien téléphoner pour moi?
voo-lay-voo byen tay-lay-faw-nay poor mwah?

**955. I want to make a local call, number
———.**
Donnez-moi la ville, numéro ———.
daw-nay-mwah la veel, new-may-roh ———.

956. Give me the long distance operator.
Donnez-moi l'Inter.
daw-nay-mwah len-tehr.

957. The operator will call you.
La téléphoniste vous rappellera.
la tay-lay-faw-neest voo ra-pehl-ra.

958. I want number ——.
Je veux le numéro ——.
zhuh vuh luh new-may-roh ——.

Note: Numbers are given in pairs.
Example: Gobelins 8995 is 89-95.

959. Hello. Allô. *a-loh.*

960. They do not answer.
On ne répond pas.
aw nuh ray-pawn pah.

961. The line is busy.
Occupé.
aw-kew-pay.

962. Hold the line, please.
Ne quittez pas, s'il vous plaît.
nuh kee-tay pah, seel voo pleh.

963. May I speak to ——?
Puis-je parler à ——?
PWEE-zhuh par-lay ah ——?

964. He is not in.
Il n'est pas ici.
eel neh pah zee-see.

965. This is —— speaking.
Ici ——.
ee-see ——.

966. Please take a message for ——.
Veuillez prendre un message pour ——.
vuh-yay PRAHN-druhn meh-sazh poor ——.

967. My number is ——.
Mon numéro est ——.
mawn new-may-roh eh ——.

968. How much is a call to ——?
Combien un appel à ——?
kawn-byen uh na-pehl ah ——?

969. There is a telephone call for you.
Il y a un coup de téléphone pour vous.
eel ya uhn koo duh tay-lay-fawn poor voo.

TELEGRAMS AND CABLEGRAMS
TÉLÉGRAMMES ET CÂBLOGRAMMES

971. Where can I send a telegram (cablegram)?
Où puis-je envoyer un télégramme (câblogramme)?
oo pwee zhahn-vwah-yay uhn tay-lay-gram (kablaw-gram)?

972. What is the rate per word to ——?
Combien par mot à ——?
kawn-byen par moh ah ——?

973. Where are the forms?
Où sont les fiches à remplir?
oo sawn lay feesh ah rahn-pleer?

974. Urgent.   When will it arrive?
Urgent.   Quand arrivera-t-il?
ewr-zhahn.   kahn tar-reev-ra-teel?

975. I wish to pay for the answer.
Je veux payer la réponse.
zhuh vuh peh-yay la ray-pawnss.

USEFUL INFORMATION: DAYS OF THE WEEK

RENSEIGNEMENTS UTILES: JOURS DE
LA SEMAINE

976. Sunday.
Dimanche.
dee-mahnsh.

977. Monday.   Tuesday.
Lundi.   Mardi.
luhn-dee.   mar-dee.

978. Wednesday.   Thursday.
Mercredi.   Jeudi.
mehr-kruh-dee.   zhuh-dee.

979. Friday.   Saturday.
Vendredi.   Samedi.
vahn-druh-dee.   sam-dee.

MONTHS, SEASONS, AND WEATHER
MOIS, SAISONS, ET TEMPS

980. January.   February.
Janvier.   Février.
zhahn-vyay.   fayv-ryay.

981. March.   April.
Mars.   Avril.
marss.   av-reel.

982. May.   June.
Mai.   Juin.
may.   zhwen.

983. July.   August.
Juillet.   Août.
zhwee-yeh.   oo.

984. September.   October.
Septembre.   Octobre.
sehp-TAHN-bruh.   awk-TAW-bruh.

985. November.   December.
Novembre.   Décembre.
naw-VAHN-bruh.   day-SAHN-bruh.

986. Spring.   Summer.
Le printemps.   L'été.
luh pren-tahn.   lay-tay.

987. Autumn.   Winter.
L'automne.   L'hiver.
law-tawn.   lee-vehr.

988. It is warm (cold).
Il fait chaud (froid).
eel feh shoh (frwah).

989. It is fair (good, bad).
Il fait clair (beau, mauvais).
eel feh klehr (boh, maw-veh).

990. It is raining (snowing).
Il pleut (neige).
eel pluh (nehzh).

991. The sun.   Sunny.   The shade.
Le soleil.   Ensoleillé.   L'ombre.
luh saw-lay.   ahn-saw-leh-yay.   LAWN-bruh.

TIME AND TIME EXPRESSIONS
HEURE

994. What time is it?
Quelle heure est-il?
keh luh reh teel?

995. It is two o'clock A.M. (P.M.).
Il est deux heures du matin (du soir).
eel eh duh zuhr dew ma-ten (dew swahr).

996. It is half past ——.
Il est —— heures et demie.
eel et —— uhr ay duh-mee.

997. It is a quarter past ——.
Il est —— heures et quart.
eel eh —— uhr ay kar.

998. It is a quarter to ——.
Il est —— heures moins le quart.
eel eh —— uhr mwen luh kar.

999. At ten minutes to ——.
À —— heures moins dix.
ah —— uhr mwen deess.

1000. At ten minutes past ——.
À —— heures dix.
ah —— uhr deess.

1001. In the morning.   In the evening.
Le matin.   Le soir.
luh ma-ten.   luh swahr.

1002. In the afternoon.   At noon.
L'après-midi.   À midi.
la-preh mee-dee.   ah mee-dee.

1003. Day.   Night.   Midnight.
Le jour.   La nuit.   Minuit.
luh zhoor.   la nwee.   mee-nwee.

1004. Yesterday.   Last night.
Hier.   Hier soir.
yehr.   yehr swahr.

1005. Today.   Tonight.   Tomorrow.
Aujourd'hui.   Ce soir.   Demain.
aw-zhoor-dwee.   suh swahr.   duh-men.

1006. The day before yesterday.
Avant-hier.
ah-vahn-tyehr.

1007. Last year.   Last month.
L'année dernière.   Le mois passé.
lan-nay dehr-nyehr.   luh mwah pas-say.

1008. Next Monday.   Next week.
Lundi prochain.   La semaine prochaine.
*luhn-dee praw-shen.   la suh-mehn praw-
shehn.*

1009. Two weeks ago.
Il y a quinze jours.
eel ya kenz zhoor.

1010. One week ago.
Il y a huit jours.
eel ya ew-ee zhoor.

1011. NUMBERS
CHIFFRES

One. Un. *uhn.*

Two. Deux. *duh.*

Three. Trois. *trwah.*

Four. Quatre. *KAH-truh.*

Five. Cinq. *senk.*

Six. Six. *seess.*

Seven. Sept. *seht.*

Eight. Huit. *ew-eet.*

Nine. Neuf. *nuhf.*

Ten. Dix. *deess.*

Eleven. Onze. *awnz.*

Twelve. Douze. *dooz.*

Thirteen. Treize. *trehz.*

Fourteen. Quatorze. *ka-tawrz.*

Fifteen. Quinze. *kenz.*

Sixteen. Seize. *sehz.*

Seventeen. Dix-sept. *dee-seht.*

Eighteen. Dix-huit. *dee-zweet.*

Nineteen. Dix-neuf. *deez-nuhf.*

Twenty. Vingt. *ven.*

Twenty-one. Vingt et un. *ven-tay-uhn.*

Twenty-two. Vingt-deux. *ven-duh.*

Thirty. Trente. *trahnt.*

Thirty-one. Trente et un. *trahn-tay-uhn.*

Forty. Quarante. *ka-rahnt.*

Fifty. Cinquante. *sen-kahnt.*

Sixty. Soixante. *swa-sahnt.*

Seventy. Soixante-dix. *swa-sahnt-deess.*

Seventy-one. Soixante-onze. *swa-sahnt-ohnz.*

Eighty. Quatre-vingts. *ka-truh-ven.*

Eighty-one. Quatre-vingt-un. *ka-truh-ven-uhn.*

Eighty-two. Quatre-vingt-deux. *ka-truh-ven-duh.*

Ninety. Quatre-vingt-dix. *ka-truh-ven-deess.*

Ninety-one. Quatre-vingt-onze. *ka-truh-ven-awnz.*

Ninety-two. Quatre-vingt-douze. *ka-truh-ven-dooz.*

One hundred. Cent. *sahn.*

Two hundred. Deux cents. *duh sahn.*

One thousand. Mille. *meel.*

Two thousand. Deux mille. *duh meel.*

First. Premier. *pruh-myay.*

Second. Deuxième. *duh-zyehm.*

Third. Troisième. *trwah-zee-ehm.*

Fourth. Quatrième. *kah-tree-ehm.*

Fifth. Cinquième. *sen-kee-ehm.*

Sixth. Sixième. *see-zee-ehm.*

Seventh. Septième. *seh-tee-ehm.*

Eighth. Huitième. *ew-ee-tee-ehm.*

Ninth. Neuvième. *nuh-vee-ehm.*

Tenth. Dixième. *dee-zee-ehm.*

1955. Mil neuf cent cinquante-cinq OR

Dix-neuf cent cinquante-cinq.
meel nuhf sahn sen-kahnt-senk OR
deess-nuhf sahn sen-kahnt-senk.

MEASUREMENTS
MESURES

1014. What is the length (width)?
Quelle est la longueur (largeur)?
keh leh la lawn-guhr (lar-zhuhr)?

1015. How much is it per meter?
Combien le mètre?
kawn-byen luh MEH-truh?

1016. What is the size?

Quelle est la pointure?

keh leh la pwen-tewr?

1017. It is ten meters long by four meters wide.

Il a dix mètres de long sur quatre mètres de large.

eel la dee MEH-truh duh lawn sewr KA-truh MEH-truh duh larzh.

1018. High. Low.

Haut. Bas.

oh. bah.

1019. Large. Small. Medium.

Grand. Petit. Moyen.

grahn. puh-tee. mwah-yen.

1020. Alike. Different.

Semblable. Différent.

sahn-BLA-bluh. dee-fay-rahn.

1021. A pair. A dozen.

Une paire. Une douzaine.

ewn pehr. ewn doo-zehn.

1022. Half a dozen.

Une demi-douzaine.

ewn duh-mee doo-zehn.

1023. Half a meter.

Cinquante centimètres.

sen-kahnt sahn-tee-MEH-truh.

COLORS
COULEURS

1026. Light. Dark.
Clair. Foncé.
klehr. fawn-say.

1027. Black. Blue. Brown.
Noir. Bleu. Brun.
nwahr. bluh. bruhn.

1028. Cream. Gray. Green.
Crème. Gris. Vert.
krehm. gree. vehr.

1029. Orange. Pink. Purple.
Orange. Rose. Violet.
aw-rahnzh. rohz. vyaw-leh.

1030. Red. White. Yellow.
Rouge. Blanc. Jaune.
roozh. blahn. zhohn.

1031. I want a lighter (darker) shade.
Je désire un ton plus clair (plus foncé).
zhuh day-zeer uhn tawn plew klehr (plew fawn-say).

COMMON OBJECTS
OBJETS COMMUNS

1033. An ash tray. Un cendrier.
uhn sahn-dree-ay.

1034. A handbag. Un sac à main.
uhn sak ah men.

1035. Boarding house. Une pension.
ewn pahn-syawn.

1036. Bobby pins. Des épingles à cheveux.
day zay-pen-gla-shuh-vuh.

1037. A box. Une boîte. *ewn bwaht.*

1038. A light bulb. Une ampoule.
ewn ahn-pool.

1039. Candy. Les bonbons. *lay bawn-bawn.*

1040. A can opener. Un ouvre-boîte.
uh noo-vruh-bwaht.

1041. Cloth. L'étoffe. *lay-tawf.*

1042. Cotton. Le coton. *luh kaw-tawn.*

1043. Silk. La soie. *la swah.*

1044. Linen. Le lin. *luh len.*

1045. Wool. La laine. *la lehn.*

1046. Cork. Le bouchon. *luh boo-shawn.*

1047. Corkscrew. Le tire-bouchon.
luh teer-boo-shawn.

1048. Cushion. Le coussin. *luh koo-sen.*

1049. Doll. La poupée. *la poo-pay.*

1050. Earrings. Les boucles d'oreille.
lay BOO-kluh daw-ray.

1051. Flashlight. La lampe électrique.
la lahn pay-lehk-treek.

1052. Glasses. Les lunettes. *lay lew-neht.*

1053. Sunglasses. Les lunettes fumées.
lay lew-neht few-may.

1054. Gold. L'or. *lawr.*

1055. Chewing gum. Le chewing gum.
luh "chewing gum".

1056. Hairnet. Le filet à cheveux.
luh fee-leh ah shuh-vuh.

1057. Hook. Le crochet. *luh kraw-sheh.*

1058. Flatiron. Le fer à repasser.
luh feh ra ruh-pas-say.

1059. Jewelry. La bijouterie.
la bee-zhoo-tree.

1060. Shoelace. Le lacet. *luh la-seh.*

1061. Leather. Le cuir. *luh kweer.*

1062. Mending cotton. Le coton à repriser.
lu'. kaw-taw na ruh-pree-zay.

1063. Mosquito net. La moustiquaire.
la moo-stee-kehr.

1064. Nail file. La lime à ongles.
la lee-ma-AWN-gluh.

1065. Necklace. Le collier. *luh kaw-lyay.*

1066. Needle. L'aiguille. *lay-GWEE-yuh.*

1067. Notebook. Le cahier. *luh ka-yay.*

1068. Padlock. Le cadenas. *luh kad-na.*

1069. Pail. Le seau. *luh soh.*

1070. Penknife. Le canif. *luh ka-neef.*

1071. Perfume. Le parfum. *luh par-fuhn.*

1072. Pin (ornamental). La broche.
la brawsh.

1073. Pin (straight). L'épingle.
lay-$\overline{PEN}$-gluh.

1074. Radio. La radio. *la rad-yoh.*

1075. Ring. La bague. *la bag.*

1076. Rubbers. Les caoutchoucs.
lay ka-oot-shoo.

1077. Safety pin. L'épingle de sûreté.
lay-P$\overline{EN}$-gluh duh sewr-tay.

1078. Scissors. Les ciseaux. *lay see-zoh.*

1079. Screw. Le vis. *luh veess.*

1080. Silver. L'argent. *lar-zhahn.*

1081. Stone (precious).
La pierre (précieuse).
la pyehr (pray-syuhz).

1082. Stopper. Le bouchon. *luh boo-shawn.*

1083. Strap. La courroie. *la koor-wah.*

1084. Straw. La paille. *la PAH-yuh.*

1085. Thimble. Le dé. *luh day.*

1086. Thread. Le fil. *luh feel.*

1087. Typewriter. La machine à écrire.
la ma-shee na ay-kreer.

1088. Umbrella. Le parapluie.
luh pa-ra-plwee.

1089. Vase. Le vase. *luh vaz.*

1090. Washcloth. Le gant de toilette.
luh ga͞hn duh twah-leht.

1091. Watch. La montre. *la M͞A͞WN-truh.*

1092. Whiskbroom. Une petite brosse.
ewn puh-teet brawss.

1093. Wire. Le fil. *luh feel.*

1094. Wood. Le bois. *luh bwah.*

1095. Wool thread. La laine à repriser.
la leh na ruh-pree-zay.

1096. Zipper. La fermeture éclair.
la fehrm-tew ray-klehr.

APPENDIX

Antibes—*ahn-teeb*

Antwerp—Anvers—*ahn-vehr*

Arles—*arl*

Avignon—*ah-veen-yawn*

Basque—*bask*

Biarritz—*bee-ah-reets*

Bordeaux—*bawr-doh*

Boulogne—*boo-LAWN-yuh*

Brittany—Bretagne—*bruh-TAN-yuh*

Brussels—Bruxelles—*brewk-sehl*

Burgundy—Bourgogne—*boor-GAWN-yuh*

Caen—*kahn*

Calais—*ka-leh*

Cannes—*kan*

Chambord—*shahn-bawr*

Chamonix—*shah-maw-nee*

Chantilly—*shahn-tee-yee*

Chenonceaux—*shuh-nawn-soh*

Chartres—*SHAR-truh*

Cherbourg—*shehr-boor*

Corsica—Corse—*kawrss*

Côte d'Azur—*koht da-zewr*

Fontainebleau—*fohn-ten-bloh*

Geneva—Genève—*zhuh-nehv*

Lausanne—*loh-zan*

Le Havre—*luh AHV-ruh*

Loire—*lwahr*

Luxembourg—*lewk-sahn-boor*

Lyons—Lyon—*lee-awn*

Marseilles—Marseille—*mar-SAY-yuh*

Meuse—*muhz*

Mont Saint-Michel—*mawn sen mee-shehl*

Nantes—*nahnt*

Nice—*neess*

Normandy—Normandie—*nawr-mahn-dee*

Paris—*pa-ree*

Reims—*renss*

Rhône—*rohn*

Riviera (the)—Riviera (la)—*reev-yeh-rah (la)*

Rouen—*roo-ahn*

Saint-Cloud—*sen cloo*

Saint-Malo—*sen ma-loh*

Seine—*sehn*

Strasbourg—*strahz-boor*

Touraine—*too-rehn*

Tours—*toor*

Versailles—*vehr-SAH-yuh*

PLACES OF INTEREST IN PARIS

L'Arc de Triomphe—*lark duh tree-awnf*

Le Bois de Boulogne—*luh bwah duh boo-LAWN-yuh*

Le Palais de Chaillot—*luh pa-leh duh shah-yoh*

La Conciergerie—*la kawn-see-ehr-zhree*

Les Halles—*lay ahl*

L'Hôtel des Invalides—*loh-tel day zen-vah-leed*

Ile de la Cité—*eel duh la see-tay*

Le Louvre—*luh LOOV-ruh*

La Madeleine—*la mad-lehn*

Montparnasse—*mawn-pahr-nass*

Montmartre—*mawn-MAR-truh*

Le Musée de Cluny—*luh mew-zay duh klew-nee*

Notre-Dame, La Cathédrale de—*naw-truh-DAHM, la ka-tay-drahl duh*

L'Opéra—*loh-pay-rah*

Le Palais de Justice—*luh pa-leh duh zhew-steess*

Le Palais du Luxembourg—*luh pa-leh dew lewk-sahn-boor*

Le Palais-Royal—*luh pa-leh-rwah-yal*

Le Panthéon—*luh pahn-tay-awn*

La Place de la Concorde—*la plass duh la kawn-kawrd*

La Place Vendôme—*la plass vahn-dohm*

Les Quais—*lay kay*

Le Quartier latin—*luh kart-yay la-ten*

Sacré-Cœur, Basilique du—*sak-ray-kuhr, ba-zee-leek dew*

La Sainte-Chapelle—*la sent-shah-pehl*

La Salle Luxembourg—*la sal lewk-sahn-boor*

La Sorbonne—*la sawr-bawn*
Le Théâtre français—*luh tay-AH-truh frahn-seh*
La Tour Eiffel—*la toor ay-fehl*
Les Tuileries—*lay twee-luh-ree*

PROPER NAMES (*The English equivalent is given in parenthesis where it is not obvious.*)

Adèle—*ah-dehl*

Adrien—*ah-dree-en̄*

Aimée—*ay-may*

Ambroise—*ahn-brwahz*

Amédée—*ah-may-day* (Amadeus)

Amélie—*ah-may-lee*

Àndré—*ahn-dray* (Andrew)

Anne—*an*

Antoine—*ahn-twan*

Antoinette—*ahn-twa-neht*

Arabelle—*ah-rah-behl*

Arnaud—*ahr-noh* (Arnold)

Arthur—*ar-tewr*

Auguste—*oh-gewst*

Baudouin—*boh-dwen̄* (Baldwin)

Benoît—*buh-nwah* (Benedict)

Berthe—*BEHR-tuh*

Bertrand—*behr-trahn̄*

Blanche—*blāhnsh*

Brigitte—*bree-zheet*

Catherine—*kah-treen*

Cécile—*say-seel*

César—*say-zahr*

Charles—*sharl*

Chrétien—*kray-tyen̄*

Christophe—*kree-stawf*

Claire—*klehr*

Claude—*klohd*

Claudine—*kloh-deen*

Clément—*klay-mahn*
Constance—*kawn-stahns*
Denis—*duh-nee*
Denise—*duh-neez*
Dominique—*daw-mee-neek*
Dorothée—*daw-raw-tay*
Edmond—*ayd-mawn*
Édouard—*ayd-wahr*
Élise—*ay-leez*
Émilie—*ay-mee-lee*
Emme—*ehm*
Étienne—*ayt-yehn* (Stephen)
Eugène—*uh-zhehn*
Eugénie—*uh-zhay-nee*
Eustache—*uh-stash* (Eustace)
Flore—*flawr*
François—*frahn-swah* (Francis)
Françoise—*frahn-swahz* (Frances)
Frédéric—*fray-day-reek*
Gautier—*goht-yay* (Walter)
Grégoire—*gray-gwahr*
Guillaume—*ghee-yohm* (William)
Hélène—*ay-lehn*
Henri—*ahn-ree*
Henriette—*ahn-ree-eht*
Isabelle—*ee-za-behl*
Jacques—*zhak* (James)
Jean—*zhahn* (John)
Jeanne—*zhan* (Joan)
Jérôme—*zhay-rohm*
Jules—*zhewl*

Julie—*zhew-lee*
Laure—*lawr*
Laurent—*law-rahn* (Lawrence)
Léon—*lay-awn*
Louis—*loo-wee*
Louise—*loo-weez*
Lucien—*lew-syen*
Madeleine—*mad-lehn*
Margot—*mahr-goh*
Marguerite—*mahr-guh-reet*
Marie—*ma-ree*
Maurice—*maw-reess*
Michel—*mee-shehl*
Olivier—*aw-leev-yay* (Oliver)
Patrice—*pa-treess* (Patrick)
Paul—*pawl*
Pierre—*pyehr* (Peter)
Raoul—*rah-ool* (Ralph)
René—*ruh-nay*
Robert—*raw-behr*
Sophie—*saw-fee*
Suzanne—*sew-zan*
Thérèse—*tay-rehz*
Thibaud—*tee-boh* (Theobald)
Valérie—*vah-lay-ree*
Vincent—*ven-sahn*

ALPHABET

A	*ah*	N	*ehn*
B	*bay*	O	*oh*
C	*say*	P	*pay*
D	*day*	Q	*kew*
E	*uh*	R	*air*
F	*ehf*	S	*ess*
G	*zhay*	T	*tay*
H	*ahsh*	U	*ew*
I	*ee*	V	*vay*
J	*zhee*	W	*DOO-bluh vay*
K	*kah*	X	*eeks*
L	*ehl*	Y	*ee-grek*
M	*ehm*	Z	*zehd*

FRENCH FOOD
and
WINE SUPPLEMENT

FRENCH FOOD SUPPLEMENT

A visit to France can be your introduction to the imagination, spirit and tradition of the French cuisine. France is very rich in natural resources and all these resources have been used creatively. In less abundant regions, dishes are prepared using foods and ingredients that are relatively unknown and unpopular in this country. Ingredients are extensive, seasonings are subtle and regional resources are developed to the utmost. French dining is not only enhanced by the art of cooking but also by the complementary art of serving. There is a pride and joy in cooking and serving—whether it be of a simple or complex nature— that is at once noticeable. To understand the spirit and tradition of French cooking and dining is to begin to understand the spirit of the French people.

Breakfast in France is quite simple. It has come to be known as the continental breakfast; but in France more accurately *café complet* consists of freshly baked *croissants*, *brioches* or French bread served with butter and jelly and *café au lait*, that is, coffee with hot milk. Lunch , usually served between 12 and 2 o'clock, is frequently the main meal of the day. It is a leisurely meal and carefully planned. Dinner is customarily served between 7 and 9 o'clock and is as significant as the mid-day meal. Wines are, of course, served with all meals; whether it be an ordinary table wine or a carefully chosen vintage wine, drinking wine is considered a natural complement for the full enjoyment of food.

The list that follows is by no means complete but is

meant to serve as an introduction to the tourist to what may at first appear to be a bewildering French menu. Dishes are alphabetized according to the French and usually appear as they would on a French menu. Descriptions are necessarily brief and have been written for the purposes of rapid reference.

Note on Hors D'Oeuvres

The preparation and serving of hors d'œuvres can be quite simple or very elaborate but it remains an essential part of the French cuisine. The custom of serving cold or hot hors d'œuvres for lunch and dinner is traditional on all French menus. Interesting and imaginative combinations of fish, shellfish, salads, eggs, vegetables, meats and marinated dishes are usually included and served in small tasteful combinations. We have not included a list of the extensive hors d'œuvres possible for the purpose of this "Native Food List." Listed simply as HORS D'ŒUVRES on the menu, this dish varies daily with the spirit of the chef, and the quality of the restaurant you choose to dine in. It is usually an adventure in the tradition of French dining.

A NOTE ON FRENCH WINES

France is renowned for producing a great variety of wines and for producing wines of good quality. Viticulture is an ancient and respected art in France and French wine growers are concerned with maintaining the quality of their product. The authenticity and quality of the wine is also guaranteed by the laws, known as *Appellation Contrôlée* or *Appellation d'Origine*, which regulate the entire process of wine production in most areas of the country. These laws ensure that the wine label accurately identifies the contents of the bottle.

The wine laws governing the production of wine in a specific vineyard are stricter than the laws controlling the production of wine in larger areas. Therefore, a wine label which indicates a specific vineyard of origin suggests a wine of a higher quality than a label which denotes only a region or district of origin. This is why the first-quality, famous French wines are always bottled under the name of a specific vineyard.

When you are traveling through France do not feel that you should drink only the great wines. Most of these wines are readily available in the United States whereas many delightful local wines are not. The local wines will be pleasant, inexpensive and unique and will add to the pleasures of dining in France.

"Wine rules" are the result of much loving experimentation by food and wine connoisseurs and are not meant to be social dictates. One should feel free to experiment, but the time-honored "rules" are often helpful.

An elementary rule-of-thumb concerning the serving of wine with food is that red wines complement red meats and white and rosé wines complement fish, shellfish, chicken and the lighter meats, such as veal. Champagne is considered an excellent dinner wine and goes well with almost any dish.

General Suggestions for Selecting Dinner Wines:

With	*Try*
Chicken Fish Shellfish Light meats (veal)	Dry white wine or rosé. Chablis is particularly good with oysters.
Red meats Game, cheese	Full-bodied red wines, i.e., Burgundy, Bordeaux or Rhône.
Turkey	Dry red or white wine.
Sweet dessert Fruit	Sweet white wine, i.e., Sauternes or Barsac. Extra dry champagne is also good.

WINE LIST

Apéritifs

It is customary in France to take a leisurely apéritif (an alcoholic wine drink), rather than a strong cocktail, to stimulate the appetite before the dinner. Popular apéritifs are:

Byrrh.
Medium dry, ruby red wine with body and subtle flavor.

Campari.
Very dry, rather bitter white wine from Italy.

Dubonnet.   Rich red, slightly sweet wine.

Pernod.
Pale green liqueur with a distinctive anisette flavor. Served with water and ice.

Sherry.
Amber colored wine from Spain.   Dry, light varieties are best served before dinner or with dinner.

Vermouth.
Red (sweet) or white (dry) wine interestingly flavored with aromatic herbs and bitters.   Usually served on ice with a twist of lemon peel.

Vermouth-cassis.
Vermouth and cassis (a sirupy liqueur made from black currants) in a pleasant tasting mixture with ice and vichy water.

Red and White Table Wines

Alsatian wines.   White wines similar to Rhine wines, produced in three different types.

    Riesling.   Dry white wine.

    Traminer.
    Medium dry wine with a pronounced spicy or fruity flavor and renowned bouquet.

    Sylvaner.   Mild, pleasant white wine.

Barsac.   Sweet, rich white wine of delicate aroma. Generally used as a dessert wine.

Bordeaux.   Also referred to as claret.   Red wines comparable in quality to Burgundy, but drier and lighter with elegant bouquet and flavor.   The following districts produce excellent claret:

    Saint-Émilion.
    Full-bodied and robust wines with strong bouquet.

Pomerol.
Somewhat lighter wines, but otherwise similar to Saint-Émilion.

Médoc.
Typical claret. Light-bodied, mellow with long lasting taste.

Burgundy.   Full-bodied dry wine of excellent color, flavor and strong bouquet.   Produced in both red and white varieties.   Some popular and generally available Burgundies are:

Nuits-Saint-Georges.
Red, very full-bodied with remarkable bouquet.

Pommard.
Somewhat lighter and more delicate.

Beaujolais.
Fresh, light red Burgundy with an earthy bouquet. Excellent when drunk young.

Chablis.
Very dry, light white wine with a peculiar "steely" flavor.

Champagne.   The best sparkling wine in the world, produced in white and pink varieties.   Champagne is made in varying degrees of sweetness and types:

Brut.   Very dry.

Extra Sec (Extra Dry).   Semi-dry.

Sec.   Less dry, actually rather sweet.

Blanc de blancs.   Extremely light and effervescent.

Rhône.   Full-bodied red wines of strong bouquet. Popular varieties are:

Côte-Rôtie.

Châteauneuf-du-Pape.

Rosé. Light, refreshing pink wines which are excellent when drunk young. The most popular rosé wines are:

Tavel. Dry, rather tart, highly praised wine.

Provence. Light, fresh and fruity wine.

Sauternes. Sweet, rich white wine. Generally used as a dessert wine.

Brandies, Liqueurs, Cordials

Brandies.

Armagnac. Superior French brandy.

Calvados. Very fine apple brandy.

Cognac.
The very best brandy in the world, originating from the district of Cognac.

Framboise.
Delicious, rich, colorless brandy made from distilled raspberries.

Mirabelle.
Alsatian brandy made from yellow plums.

Kirsch. Dry, colorless brandy made from dark, sour cherries and characterized by a piquant, slightly bitter almond flavor.

Liqueurs and cordials. (Sweetened, flavored and sometimes artificially colored.)

Benedictine.
Amber-colored liqueur made with a variety of herbs and characterized by its delicacy.

Chartreuse.
Made with a cognac base and with a mixture of many aromatic herbs. There are green and yellow varieties of this unusual liqueur, the green containing more alcohol than the yellow.

Cointreau.
Colorless, rich liqueur of subtle orange flavor.

Crème de menthe.
Strongly peppermint flavored liqueur which is available in luminous green or colorless varieties.

Grand Marnier.
Strongly orange-flavored liqueur made with a cognac base.

Beers

Bière blonde.   Light beer or ale.

Bière brune.   Dark beer or stout.

Guide to Vintages

Recent good and great vintage years. Dates in italics indicate great years, whereas roman dates indicate exceptionally good years.

Alsatian wine: *1959*, 1958, 1957, 1955, *1953*

Red Burgundy: *1959*, 1958, 1957, 1955, 1953, 1952, 1949, *1947*, *1945*, 1934, *1929*

White Burgundy: *1959*, 1958, 1957, 1955, 1953, 1952, 1950, 1949, *1947*, 1945

Bordeaux (Claret): *1959*, 1958, 1957, 1955, 1953, 1952, 1949, *1947*, *1945*, 1934, *1929*

Rhône wines: *1959*, 1958, 1957, 1955, 1952, 1949, *1947*, *1945*

Champagne: 1959, 1958, 1957, 1955, 1953, 1952, 1949, *1947*

Sauternes and Barsac: *1959*, 1958, 1953, 1952, 1949, *1947*, *1945*, 1937, 1934, *1929*

Glossary of General Wine Terms

Vin blanc.   White wine.

Vin borru.
Light young Burgundy often available in restaurants by the glass.

Vin doux.   Sweet wine.

Vin fin.   Fine wine.

Vin gris.   Rosé wine of Alsace.

Vin jaune.
Yellowish-amber colored wine resembling a dry sherry in flavor and bouquet.

Vin mousseux.   Sparkling wine.

Vin ordinaire.   Ordinary table wine.

Vin de paille.
"Straw" wine, gray-pink in color. A sweet, rich dessert wine.

Vin du pays.   Regional or local wine.

Vin rosé.   Pink wine.

Vin rouge.   Red wine.

Vin sec.   Dry wine.

USEFUL MENU TERMS

L'addition.   The check.
À la carte OR **carte.**
A list of individual dishes at a fixed price.
À prix fixe.   At a fixed price.
Carte du jour.   Menu or bill of fare.
Couvert.   Cover charge.
Déjeuner.   Luncheon.
Dîner.   Dinner.
Petit déjeuner.   Breakfast.
Inclusif.   Included.
Plat.   A single course or dish.
Selon grosseur OR **S.G.**   According to size.
Service compris.   Service charge included.
Sommelier.   Wine steward.
Spécialités.   Specialties.
Supplément.   Additional charge.
Sur commande.   On special order.
Table d'hôte. The house lunch or dinner
at a fixed price.

STYLES OF PREPARATION:
SOME GENERAL TERMS

À la . . .   In the style of . . .
À l'andalouse.
Served with green peppers and tomatoes.

130

À l'africaine.   Served with rice.

À l'anglaise.   Boiled.

À l'aubergiste.
Prepared in the customary style of the restaurant or inn.

À l'autrichienne.
Austrian style; seasoned with paprika and caraway seeds.

À la grecque.   Greek style with olive oil.

À la minute.   Quickly prepared.

À la mode de . . .   In the style of . . .

À la russe.   With sour cream.

À point.
Used to describe the preparation of meat as medium or done to a turn.

Assorti.   Assorted.

Au gratin.
Baked in a cream sauce with a garnish of cheese and bread crumbs.

Au jus.   With natural juice of the beef.

Au kirsch.   Mixed with the brandy, kirsch.   Usually refers to fresh fruit.

Au lait.   With milk.

Au maigre.   Meatless dish.

Au vin rouge.   Prepared with red wine.

Bellevue.
Served in aspic accompanied by a white sauce garnished with truffles, tongue and tarragon.

Bien cuit.   Well done.

Blanchi.   Blanched.

Bouilli.   Boiled.

Bourgeoisie.
Cooked in hearty family style with carrots, onions, potatoes and bacon.

Braisé. Braised.

Brochette.
Meat or fish and vegetables grilled on a skewer over the open fire.

Brouillé. Scrambled.

Canapé.
Small, daintily prepared open sandwich served as an appetizer.

Casserole.
Food served in an individual dish.

Charolais. Charcoal broiled.

Châtelaine.
Garnish of artichoke hearts, tomatoes and small roast potatoes.

Chiffonade. Served with shredded vegetables.

Cocotte. Served in an individual earthenware or copper pot.

Confiserie. Sweets and candies.

Croûton.
Diced toast fried in butter or oil and used for soups, salads and garnish.

Désossé. Boneless.

Diable. Deviled. Prepared in highly seasoned style.

Dolmas.
Chopped liver or other meat and vegetables wrapped in vine leaves, cabbage leaves or peppers.

Émincé. Minced meat dish served with a seasoned sauce.

En papillote.
Baked in an oiled paper bag to allow steaming in natural juices.

Entremets.   Additional course after the roast .

Escalope.   Thinly sliced meat.

Étuvé.   Stewed.

Farci.   Stuffed.

Flambé.   Served flaming in rum or brandy.

Frit.   Fried.

Galantine.
Rolled or pressed meat or poultry prepared with stock and gelatine and served cold. Usually a buffet or luncheon dish.

Gelé.   Jellied.

Glacé.   Iced.

Gratiné.   Served with bread crumbs or cheese.

Grillade.   A grilled dish .

Grillé.   Grilled or broiled.

Haché.   Chopped or sliced.

Hachis.   Hash.

Hongroise.
Hungarian style; prepared with sour cream and paprika.

Indienne.   Curried.

Jardinière.
Fresh vegetables attractively cut and used as a garnish.

Julienne.   Cut in thin strips.

Lyonnaise.   Served with onions.

Macédoine.   Combination of cut up fruits or vegetables.

Macéré.   Pickled.

Nature OR **au naturel.**   Plain, uncooked.

Panaché.   Mixed.

Pané.   Prepared with bread crumbs.

Parmentier.   Prepared with potatoes.

Pâté.
Creamy paste made with fish, poultry or meat and distinctively seasoned.

Paysanne.   Country style; a regional preparation.

Printanière.
Garnished with diced spring vegetables.

Provençale.
Prepared with oil, vinegar, herbs, garlic.   Served hot or cold.

Purée.   Mashed or strained.

Quenelle.
Oval shaped balls made with chopped chicken, veal or fish and seasonings.

Ragoût.   Stew.

Rissoles OR **rissolettes.**
Minced meat fried in a thin pastry.

Rochambeau.
Garnish of carrots, lettuce and cauliflower.

Saignant.·   Rare.

Saumuré.   Pickled or marinated.

Sauré.   Cured in smoke.

Sauté.   Gently browned in butter.

Timbale.
Traditional French mould for baking and preparing hot or cold desserts.

Véronique.   Garnished with grapes.

Viande fumée.   Smoked meat.

SAUCES AND CONDIMENTS

Allemande.
White sauce made with veal stock, egg yolk, lemon juice and seasonings.

Anchois.   Anchovy sauce.

Aurore.   Chicken and tomato sauce.

Béarnaise.
Subtly seasoned sauce made with butter, shallots, egg yolks, tarragon and wine.

Béchamel.   Thick, creamy white sauce.

Bercy.
Sauce made with fish stock, wine and shallots.

Beurre blanc.   White butter sauce.

Beurre fondu.   Melted butter sauce.

Beurre noir.
Browned butter with vinegar and parsley.

Beurre roux.   Browned butter sauce.

Bigarrade.
Duck stock, orange and lemon juice and rind combined in a sauce for duckling.

Bolognaise.
Spicy sauce prepared with garlic, tomatoes, vegetables and seasonings.

Bonne femme.   Rich, creamy sauce.

Bordelaise.
Wine sauce made with stock, seasonings, shallots and wine.

Bourguignonne.
Wine sauce made with onions, spices, beef stock and red wine.

Bretonne.
Fish sauce made with fish stock, leek, celery, beans and mushrooms.

Câpre.
Caper sauce made with fish stock, butter and capers; served with fish.

Cardinal.   Béchamel sauce and red lobster butter.

Chasseur.
Butter or olive oil, mushrooms, tomato sauce, meat glaze combined with white wine and brandy.

Créole.
Sauce made with onions, tomatoes, peppers for rice.

Diable.
Hot, spicy sauce made with wine, vinegar, fresh pepper and shallots.

Duglère.
Rich creamy sauce made with fish stock, butter, eggs, cream, wine and tomatoes.

Espagnol.
Rich brown sauce made with meat stock, vegetables and tomatoes.

Fines herbes.
Sauce made with finely chopped herbs; usually served with fish, fowl, and omelettes.

Gastronome.   White wine sauce.

Génoise.
Cold sauce made with mayonnaise, cream and nuts.

Hollandaise.
Rich, creamy sauce made with egg yolks, butter and lemon juice, usually served with fish or vegetables.

Indienne.   Curry sauce.

Journeaux.   Chicken liver sauce.

Livornaise.   Sauce of anchovy paste, oil and eggs.

Madère.   Madeira wine sauce.

Maître d'hôtel.
Light sauce made with butter, lemon juice and parsley.

Marguery.   White wine sauce for fish and seafood.

Matelote.
Sauce of fish stock, wine, mushrooms and anchovies; usually served with fish.

Meunière.   Butter sauce.

Mornay.
Rich, cream sauce garnished with grated cheese.

Mousseline.   Creamy hollandaise sauce.

Moutarde.   Mustard.

Nantua.
Sauce made with crayfish, white wine, vegetables and tomatoes.

Newburg.
Rich sauce combining sherry, cream, egg yolks and lobster meat.

Niçoise.
Sauce made with onions, garlic, oil, tomatoes and vegetables used for fish, chicken or meat.

Normande.
Cream sauce combined with fish stock and mushrooms.

Périgueux.
Sauce made with stock, wine, tomatoes and truffles.

Périgourdine.
Rich madeira wine made with truffles and goose livers.

Piquante.   Spicy sauce.

Poivrade.
Highly seasoned sauce made with freshly ground peppercorns, onions and stock.

Portugaise.   Tomato, vegetable sauce.

Printanière.
White sauce with green vegetables and parsley.

Raifort.   Horseradish.

Ravigote.
Sauce made with wine, vinegar, stock, shallots and fresh tarragon; served hot or cold.

Régence.
White wine sauce with mushrooms and truffles.

Rouennaise.
Red wine sauce made with duck livers, bay leaves and thyme; usually served with duck.

Robert.
Spicy meat sauce made with onions, wine, meat stock or glaze, mustard and sugar.

Sabayon.
Rich frothy dessert sauce made with marsala wine, eggs, sugar whipped together and flavored to taste.

Saupiquet.   Spiced vinegar sauce.

Soubise.   Béchamel sauce with finely minced onions.

Smitane.
Sour cream sauce with sautéed onions and white wine.

Suprême.   Rich sweet cream sauce.

Tartare.
Cold, well-seasoned sauce made with mayonnaise, vinegar, mustard, pickles, herbs; usually served cold.

Verte.
Mayonnaise seasoned and colored with green vegetables.

Velouté.   Rich, creamy sauce for chicken or fish.

Vinaigrette.
Sauce or a dressing for vegetables or salads made with oil, vinegar, mustard and spices.

BREADS AND BUTTERS

Brioche.   Light, sweet, breakfast roll.

Croissant.   Flaky, crescent-shaped breakfast roll.

Pain.   Bread.

Pain doré.   French toast.

Pain grillé.   Toast.

Pain noir.   Wheat or rye bread.

Petit pain.   Roll.

Beurre.   Butter.

Beurre d'anchois.   Anchovy butter.

SOUPS

Bisque.
Rich, creamy soup made with a basic fish stock, fish or shellfish.

Bisque d'écrevisses.   Crayfish soup.

Bisque de homard.   Lobster soup.

Bisque d'huîtres.   Oyster soup.

Bouillabaisse.
Hearty fish soup much like stew made with a variety of fish, wine, tomatoes, onion, garlic, saffron, fennel and served with French bread.

Bouillabaisse à la marseillaise.
Bouillabaisse prepared with Mediterranean fish.

Bouillon.   Broth.

Consommé.
Clear broth made with chicken or meat and vegetables and served with various garnishes.

Consommé brunoise.   Clear beef soup.

Consommé vert.
Green consommé made with asparagus tips, peas, string beans, sorrel leaves and chervil.

Crème d'asperges.   Cream of asparagus soup.

Crème de carottes.   Cream of carrot soup.

Crème de champignons.   Cream of mushroom soup.

Crème d'épinards.   Cream of spinach soup.

Crème Olga.   Mushroom and onion soup.

Crème vichyssoise.
Cold, piquant soup made with potatoes and leek.

Marmite OR **petite marmite.**
Classic French soup prepared with beef, poultry, and vegetables.   Traditionally served in an earthenware pot with toasted bread and cheese.

Potage.   Soup.

Potage à l'ail.   Garlic soup served with cheese.

Potage bonne femme.   Leek and potato soup.

Potage bourguignonne.
Hearty vegetable and meat soup.

Potage cressonière.
Purée of potato and watercress soup.

Potage grand duc.   Cauliflower soup.

Potage du jour.   Particular soup prepared for the day.

Potage au lentilles.   Lentil soup.

Potage Marguerite.   Kidney bean soup.

Potage à la milanaise.
Vegetable and meat soup with cheese.

Potage parmentier.   Potato soup.

Potage portugais.   Spicy, tomato soup.

Potage à la reine.   Cream of chicken soup.

Potage au vermicelle.   Noodle soup.

Potage de volaille.   Chicken broth.

Pot-au-feu.
Traditional hearty soup similar to petite marmite.

Poule au pot. Chicken and broth served in the pot.

Soupe au chou. Cabbage soup.

Soupe aux moules. Mussel soup.

Soupe à l'oignon.
Onion soup served with toasted bread and cheese.

Soupe aux poissons. Fish soup.

Vichyssoise.
Potato and leek soup made with sour cream; served cold.

FISH AND SHELLFISH

Aigrefin. Haddock.

Arachon. French oyster.

Banquet. Prawn.

Bar de mer. Sea bass.

Blanchaille. Whitebait.

Brème. Bream. (A fish in the carp family.)

Brochet badoise.
Baked pike prepared with sour cream.

Cabillaud au four. Baked codfish.

Carpe à la polonaise.
Carp cooked in red wine with onions and almonds.

Carrelet. Flounder.

Caviar frais. Fresh caviar.

Chaudfroid de saumon.
Cold salmon in jellied sauce.

Clovisse. Clam.

Coquillages. Shellfish.

Coquilles provençale.
Scallops in a dried mushroom sauce.

Coquilles St.-Jacques.   Baked scallops au gratin.

Cotriade.   Fish stew.

Crevettes.   Shrimps.

Croustade aux langoustes.
Pastry shell filled with creamed lobster.

Darne.   Slice of fish with the bone.

Darne Montmorency.
Slice of salmon with mushrooms and olives.

Écrevisse.   Crayfish.

Escargots.   Snails.

Escargots à la bourguignonne.
Snails cooked in wine sauce and baked in well-seasoned
butter.

Esturgeon.   Sturgeon.

Féra.   Whitefish.

Filet de sole amandine.
Fillet of sole sautéed in butter sauce and garnished with
shredded almonds.

Filet de sole bonne femme.
Sole prepared in a white wine sauce and hollandaise
sauce.

Filet de sole dieppoise.
Sole prepared in a sauce of mussels and shrimps.

Filet de sole aux huîtres.
Fillet of sole poached, sautéed in butter and prepared
with oysters.

Filet de sole mâconnaise.
Sole in red wine sauce.

Filet de sole à la Mornay.
Fillet of sole with a cheese sauce.

Flet.   Flounder.

Flétan.   Halibut.

Fruits de mer.   Seafood.

Hareng.   Herring.

Hareng fumé.   Smoked herring.

Hareng mariné.   Marinated herring.

Hareng salé.   Kipper.

Hareng saur.   Red herring.

Homard.   Lobster.

Homard à l'américaine OR **armoricaine.**
Lobster meat in a rich tasty sauce of butter, stock, fresh tomatoes, wine and brandy.

Homard en bellevue OR **aspic de homard en bellevue.**   Lobster in fish aspic.

Homard à la newburg.
Lobster newburg (lobster meat in a sherry cream sauce).

Homard Marguerite.
Lobster with mushrooms and truffles in a rich cream sauce with wine.

Homard parisienne.
Cold, boiled lobster served in the shell with mayonnaise dressing.

Homard thermidor.
Lobster thermidor. (Lobster meat mixed with rich cream sauce and wine. Baked in the shell, covered with cheese and bread crumbs.)

Huîtres en cheval.
Oysters on horseback. (Oysters rolled in bacon, grilled and served on toasted bread squares.)

Huîtres en coquille.   Oysters on the half shell.

Laitance.   Fish roe.

Langouste.
Crawfish OR crayfish. (European lobster similar to American varieties.)

Langoustines.
Prawns. (A large kind of shrimps.)

Loup. Bass.

Maquereau mariné. Marinated mackerel.

Marennes. Small oysters.

Matelote. Fish stew.

Médaillons de poissons. Halibut steaks.

Merlan. Whiting.

Merluche. Dried codfish.

Morue provençale. Codfish in tomato sauce.

Moules. Mussels.

Moules bordelaise. Mussels in wine sauce.

Moules farcies. Stuffed mussels.

Moules marinière.
Mussels steamed in a wine sauce with butter and shallots.

Moules panées. Baked mussels.

Moules à la provençale.
Mussels cooked in a spicy sauce made with oil, garlic, wine, fish stock and herbs.

Œufs de poisson. Fish roe.

Palourde. Clam.

Panchouse. Fish stew made with fresh-water fish.

Perche. Perch.

Pieuvre. Octopus.

Plie. Plaice. (Similar to sole.)

Pochouse bourguignonne. Fish stew.

Poireaux aux crevettes. Shrimps with leeks.

Poisson. Fish.

Poulpe.   Octopus.

Quenelles de brochet.   Fish or meat dumplings.

Raie au beurre noir.
Sea skate sautéed in brown butter.

Rouget au fenouil.
Mediterranean fish cooked in olive oil with bacon and seasoned with fennel.

Rousette.   Variety of salmon.

Royan.   Herring.

Salmis de poissons.   Mixed seafood.

Sardines à l'huile.   Sardines in olive oil.

Sardines à la niçoise.
Sardines cooked in a white wine sauce with mushrooms and spices.

Saumon fumé.   Smoked salmon.

Saumon glacé OR **chaudefroid de saumon.**
Cold salmon in aspic.

Saumonneau.   Baby salmon.

Scampi.   Large shrimp prepared in seasoned garlic sauce.

Sole Albert.   Sole with oysters and mushrooms.

Sole arlésienne.
Sole cooked with garlic, onions, tomatoes and spices.

Sole Colbert.
Boned fillet of sole, breaded and fried.

Sole gratin.
Sole baked with bread crumbs, mushrooms and cheese.

Sole limande.   Lemon sole.

Sole Marguery.
Sole prepared with a rich, cream sauce of shrimps, mushrooms and wine.

Sole Mirabeau.   Sole with anchovy sauce.

Sole Olga.
Sole poached and stuffed into baked potatoes and garnished with a rich shrimp sauce.

Sole Orly.
Sole fried in deep fat and served with a tomato sauce.

Sole vin blanc.
Sole in a cream sauce made with wine, stock, egg yolks and cream.

Tacaud.   Variety of codfish.

Tanche.   Variety of carp.

Thon à l'huile.   Tuna fish in oil.

Truite.   Trout.

Truite au bleu.
Fresh trout poached in water and vinegar resulting in a bluish color.

Truite saumonée.   Salmon trout.

Turbatin.   Native French fish similar to flounder.

Turbot.   Fish similar to flounder.

Turbot bonne femme.
Turbot cooked in cream sauce with wine, mushrooms and shallots.

Turbot au champagne.
Turbot poached in white wine or champagne.

Vandoise.   Variety of carp.

Vangeren.   Variety of carp.

ENTRÉES : MEATS AND MISCELLANEOUS DISHES

Bifteck tartare.
Raw chopped beef usually served with an accompanying sauce.

Blanquette d'agneau.
Lamb stew with mushrooms and onions.

Blanquette de veau.
Veal stew in a rich sauce.

Bœuf à la mode.
Marinated beef braised with carrots, mushrooms and onions.

Bœuf bouilli.   Boiled beef.

Bœuf bourguignonne.
Beef stew with red wine, tomato paste, onions and mushrooms.

Bœuf en daube.   Beef stew with red wine.

Bœuf salé.   Corned beef.

Carbonnade.
Beef prepared in the oven with onions, beer and beef stock.

Carbonnade à la flamande.
Browned slices of beef cooked in seasoned beer sauce.

Carré de porc rôti.   Roast loin of pork.

Cassoulet.
Native stew made with white beans, sausage, pork, tomatoes (sauce or paste), onions, garlic and bacon rind cooked and served in casserole.

Cervelles au beurre noir.
Calves' brains served with browned butter.

Cervelles beurre noisette.
Poached brains in hazel-butter sauce.

Châteaubriand.
Thick steak cut from middle of the beef fillet.

Choucroute garni.
Hot sauerkraut served with a variety of meats and sausages.

Côte de veau.   Veal cutlet.

Côtelette de veau en papillote.
Veal cutlet baked and served in a sealed paper container.

Côtes de bœuf.   Ribs of beef.

Côtes de porc.   Spareribs.

Couchon de lait.   Suckling pig.

Cuisseau.   Leg of veal.

Daube.
Stew usually made with lamb or mutton, herbs, vegetables and wine.

Entrecôte.   Thin, rib steak.

Entrecôte chasseur.
Steak served with a wine sauce.

Entrecôte château.   Large, thick steak.

Entrecôte minute.
Very thin slice of beef steak for quick broiling.

Épaule de veau.   Shoulder of veal.

Escalopes de veau.   Thin slices of veal.

Escalopes de veau panées.
Thinly sliced veal, lightly breaded and fried and garnished with lemon and chopped egg.

Escalopes de veau à la royale.
Sliced veal in brandied cream sauce.

Estouffade.
Braised beef with wine, stock, onions, garlic, herbs and mushrooms.

Estouffade de bœuf.
Beef stew with red wine and onions.

Estouffade aux haricots.
Stew of sausage, pork and white beans.

Filet de bœuf.
Fillet of beef; one of the choicest cuts.

Filet mignon. Choice fillet of beef.

Filet de porc. Pork fillet.

Filets de veau. Veal fillets.

Foie à la bordelaise.
Liver with wine and mushrooms.

Foie gras.
Finely ground goose liver mixed with chicken force-meat, truffles, salt, pepper and brandy. Served hot or cold as a delicacy.

Foie à la provençale.
Liver sautéed in garlic butter.

Foie de veau. Calf's liver.

Foie de veau moissonière.
Calf's liver with onions, herbs and red wine.

Foie de volaille. Chicken liver.

Fricadelles.
Meat patties made with chopped beef, onions and seasoning.

Fricandeau. Sliced meat in wine sauce.

Fricassée de veau. Veal stew.

Gigot d'agneau. Leg of lamb.

Gigot de mouton. Leg of mutton.

Goulasch de veau. Veal goulash.

Grenouilles sautées fines herbes.
Frog's legs sautéed in butter with finely chopped herbs and lemon.

Haricots de mouton.
Mutton stew with beans, onions and carrots.

Jambon. Ham.

Jambon à la crème. Ham in cream sauce.

Jambon au madère.
Ham in madeira wine sauce.

Langue de bœuf.   Ox tongue.

Langue de veau.   Calf's tongue.

Navarin de mouton.   Mutton stew.

Noisettes d'agneau.   Boneless lamb chops.

Paupiette.
Large slice of meat, rolled and stuffed with forcemeat and baked.

Paupiette de veau.
Slice of veal, stuffed and rolled.

Petit salé.   Salt or pork bacon.

Pied de veau.   Calf's feet grilled or baked.

Plat de côtes au chou.
Boiled beef and cabbage.

Poitrine de veau.   Breast of veal.

Pot-au-feu.
Boiled beef with vegetables; served in the pot.

Potée limousine.
Stew of pork, cabbage and chestnuts.

Pré salé.
Lamb fed in salt marshes causing its distinctive taste; a regional specialty of Normandy.

Quenelles.
Dumpling stuffed with a tasty preparation of minced meat or fish.

Queue de bœuf.   Ox tail.

Quiche Lorraine.
Open-baked pie filled with a mixture of chopped ham or bacon, beaten eggs, cream, cheese.

Ragoût d'agneau.   Lamb stew.

Ragoût de bœuf.   Beef stew.

Ragoût de mouton jardinière.
Mutton stew with finely cut carrots, turnips, onions, potatoes and peas.

Ris d'agneau.   Lamb sweetbreads.

Ris de veau.   Veal sweetbreads.

Rognons de mouton.   Sheep kidneys.

Rognons de veau.   Veal kidneys.

Saucisse.   Fresh pork sausage.

Saucisson.   Smoked pork sausage.

Sauté de bœuf.   Beef sautéed in a wine, tomato sauce.

Selle d'agneau.   Saddle of lamb.

Selle de veau.   Saddle of veal.

Steak à l'américaine.
Grilled steak served with a fried egg.

Steak de cheval.   Horsemeat steak.

Steak Diane.   Very thin steak.

Steak haché.   Chopped steak.

Steak au poivre.
Choice cut of steak covered with freshly crushed peppercorns, melted butter and then broiled.

Tendrons de veau.   Braised veal.

Terrine maison.
Finely ground mixture of chicken, goose liver, pork and distinctive seasonings; very often a regional specialty.

Tournedos.
Center cut of beef or a small thick fillet, sautéed or grilled and garnished in many different ways.

Tournedos à la béarnaise.
Grilled fillet of beef served with béarnaise sauce.

Tournedos chasseur.
Beef fillet cooked in butter and garnished with a sauce of mushrooms, tomatoes and wine.

Tournedos Rossini.
Grilled fillet of beef garnished with goose liver, truffles and a wine sauce.

Tranche de bœuf.   Slice of steak.

Tripe à la mode.
Tripe cooked with tomatoes, shallots and apple brandy.

Veau.   Veal.

Veau Marengo.
Sliced veal sautéed in olive oil with wine, mushrooms, tomatoes.

Veau mimosa.
Veal with port wine and fresh tarragon.

POULTRY AND GAME

Aguillettes de caneton.   Breast of duckling.

Ailerons de poulet.   Chicken wings.

Bécasse.   Woodcock.

Bécassine.   Snipe.

Brochettes de foies de volaille.
Skewer of chicken livers brushed with butter and grilled on an open flame.

Cailles.   Quails.

Canard.   Duck.

Canard Montmorency.
Duck cooked in a rich sauce made with whole bing cherries.

Canard aux olives.
Duck prepared in a sauce with olives.

Canard à la presse.
Pressed duck served in flaming brandy.

Canard sauvage. Wild duck.

Caneton. Duckling.

Caneton aux cerises. Duckling with cherries.

Caneton à l'orange.
Duckling with orange sauce.

Caneton aux pommes.
Roast duckling with apples.

Caneton rouennais.
Duckling served with a rich sauce made with duck stock, cognac, red wine and onions.

Caneton sauvage. Wild duckling.

Civet de lièvre à la française.
Hare cooked in a red wine sauce with mushrooms and onions.

Civette. Hare stew.

Coq à la bourguignonne.
Rooster simmered with wine, brandy, salt pork, onions, mushrooms and a bouquet of herbs.

Coq au vin.
Chicken cooked in wine, brandy, onions and mushrooms.

Côtelettes de poulet. Chicken cutlets.

Cou d'oie farci. Stuffed goose neck.

Crêpes niçoises.
Pancake stuffed with a tasty chicken preparation.

Crochettes de volaille. Chicken croquettes.

Croustade de volaille.
Pastry shells filled with well-seasoned minced chicken.

Dinde. Turkey.

Dindonneau. Young turkey.

Faisan.   Pheasant.

Filets de poulets.   Breasts of chicken.

Foies de volaille et rognons au vin rouge.
Chicken livers and kidneys sautéed in red wine.

Fricassée de poulet.   Chicken fricassee.

Galantine de volaille.
Chicken served in a decorative mould; made with chicken stock and gelatin.

Ganga.   Species of grouse.

Gelinotte.   Hazel hen (a game bird).

Grand coq de bruyère.   Grouse.

Grive.   Thrush.

Lapereau.   Young rabbit.

Lapin.   Rabbit.

Lapin chasseur.
Rabbit stew with wine, tomatoes, mushrooms and herbs.

Lièvre.   Hare.

Lièvre à la royale.
Hare stew made with wine, vinegar, carrots, onions and garlic.

Marcassin.   Young boar.

Merles.   Blackbirds; usually roasted.

Oie OR **oison.**
Goose.

Ortolans.
Small delicate birds; prepared as a table delicacy.

Pain de volaille froid.   Cold chicken loaf.

Pâté d'alouettes.   Lark pie.

Pâté de cailles.   Quail pie.

Pâté de poulet.
Pâté of chicken made with chicken, truffles, brandy, seasoning, forcemeat and enclosed in puff pastry and baked.

Perdreau. Partridge.

Perdrix. Partridge.

Pigeonneaux OR **pigeons.** Squabs.

Poularde.*
A hen or fat pullet especially fattened for the kitchen.

Poularde en brioche.
Chicken baked in yeast dough.

Poularde en chemise.
Poached stuffed chicken.

Poularde à l'estragon.
Chicken prepared with fresh tarragon.

Poularde de grain.* Spring chicken.

Poularde lyonnaise.
Stuffed chicken cooked with truffles and vegetables.

Poularde Marengo.
Chicken dish made with olive oil, wine, stock, fresh tomatoes or tomato paste, and black olives.

Poularde à la Périgord.
Chicken stuffed with truffles and baked in a glazed sauce.

Poularde au riz.
Well-seasoned chicken garnished with rice.

Poularde strasbourgeoise.
Chicken breasts stuffed with pâté de fois gras.

---

* Strictly speaking *poularde* is a fat pullet, *poularde de grain* is a spring chicken, *poule* is a hen, *poulet* is a chicken, and *poussin* is a very young chicken. All of these terms tend to be used rather loosely for the extensive variety of chicken dishes.

Poularde à la tartare.
Chicken brushed with olive oil, bread crumbs usually served with a sauce.

Poularde en terrine à la gelée.
Chicken stuffed with forcemeat, prepared in an aspic and usually served on ice for hors d'œuvres or cold buffet.

Poularde vin blanc.   Chicken with white wine.

Poule* au pot.   Chicken in the pot.

Poulet.*   Young chicken.

Poulet amandine.
Chicken cooked in a wine sauce with tomatoes, stock, sour cream and garnished with shredded almonds.

Poulet armagnac.
Chicken cooked in a sauce with armagnac brandy.

Poulet bourguignonne.
Chicken cooked in red wine with onions and mushrooms.

Poulet chasseur.
Chicken sautéed in olive oil, butter, shallots and tomato sauce.

Poulet à la crème.
Chicken in a rich cream sauce.

Poulet dinde.   Baby turkey.

Poulet de grain en casserole.
Spring chicken cooked and served in a casserole; usually in a wine sauce with onions, carrots, turnips, celery, leeks and mushrooms.

Poulet de grain grillé diable.
Broiled deviled spring chicken; sautéed in butter, brushed with mustard, bread crumbs.

* See footnote p. 37.

Poulet grillé. Grilled chicken.

Poulet à la Kiev.
Boned chicken breasts, stuffed with a finger of sweet butter and fried.

Poulet à la king.
Chicken à la king; sautéed chicken served in a cream sauce with mushrooms and grated cheese.

Poulet Marengo.
Chicken sautéed in olive oil with wine, mushrooms, stock, tomatoes and olives.

Poulet niçoise.
Chicken cooked with garlic, saffron and tomatoes.

Poulet paysanne. Chicken with vegetables.

Poulet sauté. Chicken lightly cooked in butter.

Poulet sauté aux fines herbes.
Sautéed chicken seasoned with parsley, chevril and tarragon.

Poulet sauté indienne. Curried chicken.

Poulet sauté à la Maintenon.
Sautéed chicken with mushrooms.

Poulet sauté provençale.
Chicken sautéed in olive oil and simmered in a well-seasoned wine sauce with herbs.

Poulet à la Stanley.
Chicken with mushrooms and paprika.

Poussin. Very young chicken.

Quenelle de volaille. Chicken dumpling.

Salade de poulet. Chicken salad.

Salmis. Birds or game birds stewed in wine.

Sanglier. Boar.

Selle de chevreuil.
Saddle of roebuck; usually served with a sauce.

Soufflé de volaille. Chicken soufflé.

Suprêmes de poulet. Breasts of chicken.

Suprêmes de volaille aux champignons.
Sautéed chicken breasts served with mushrooms in a
delicately seasoned sauce with varied garnishes.

Suprêmes de volaille jardinière.
Sautéed chicken breasts served with a garnish of fresh
vegetables.

Suprêmes de volaille parisienne.
Sautéed chicken cooked in a wine sauce and served
with a rich mushroom sauce or hollandaise.

Venado. Venison.

Vol-au-vent.
Light puff pastry filled with chicken or meat in a rich,
cream sauce.

OMELETS

Omelette aux artichauts.
Omelet with artichoke hearts.

Omelette au lard.   Omelet with bacon.

Omelette bonne femme.
Bacon and onion omelet.

Omelette célestine. Jam omelet.

Omelette aux cèpes. Sliced mushroom omelet.

Omelette aux champignons.
Mushroom omelet.

Omelette au confiture. Jam omelet.

Omelette aux crevettes. Shrimp omelet.

Omelette espagnole. Spanish omelet.

Omelettes aux fines herbes.
Omelet with finely chopped herbs.

Omelette foies de volaille.
Omelet with sautéed chicken livers.

Omelette au fromage.   Cheese omelet.

Omelette au jambon.   Ham omelet.

Omelette au lard.   Bacon omelet.

Omelette à la lyonnaise.
Omelet with finely minced sautéed onions.

Omelette nature.   Plain omelet.

Omelette aux oignons.   Chopped onion omelet.

Omelette Parmentier.   Diced potato omelet.

Omelette aux pommes de terre.
Potato omelet.

Omelette provençale.
Omelet made with onions, garlic and tomatoes.

Omelette aux rognons.   Kidney omelet.

Omelette à la Rossini.
Omelet made with foie gras and truffles.

Omelette soufflée.
Light, puffed omelet; usually a luncheon or dessert dish.

Omelette aux tomates.   Tomato omelet.

POTATOES

Pommes de terre allemande.
Cooked potatoes, sliced and fried in butter.

Pommes de terre allumettes.
Fried, shoe-string potatoes.

Pommes de terre Alphonse.
Cooked potatoes, sliced and mixed with diced sweet peppers, brushed with maître d'hôtel butter (butter with parsley and dash of lemon juice) and baked with grated cheese.

Pomme de terre à l'anglaise.
Peeled boiled potato.

Pommes de terre Anna.
Sliced potatoes baked and browned in butter in the oven.

Pomme de terre bouillée.   Boiled potato.

Pommes de terre boulangère.
Quartered potatoes baked with minced, sautéed onions.

Pommes de terre "chip."
Thin, crisp fried potato chips.

Pommes de terre à la crème.
Creamed potatoes.

Pommes de terre dauphine.
Sliced potatoes baked with butter and grilled Swiss cheese.

Pommes de terre duchesse.
Boiled potatoes, mashed with egg yolks and butter, shaped into patties and fried or baked.

Pommes de terre farcies.   Stuffed potatoes.

Pommes de terre au four.   Baked potatoes.

Pommes de terre frites.   French fried potatoes.

Pommes de terre hongroise.
Sliced potatoes with onion, paprika, moistened with bouillon and baked.

Pommes de terre au lard.
Potatoes fried with bacon.

Pommes de terre Lorette.
Mashed potatoes mixed with eggs and butter, shaped into crescents and deep fat fried.

Pommes de terre lyonnaise.
Cooked, sliced potatoes sautéed with sliced onions.

Pommes de terre Macaire.
Baked potatoes mashed and prepared in pancake style and browned in an omelet pan of hot butter.

Pommes de terre maître d'hôtel.
Sliced potatoes cooked in milk and served with chopped parsley.

Pommes de terre marquise.
Cooked potatoes with tomato purée shaped into patties and sautéed in butter.

Pommes de terre mousseline.
Cooked mashed potatoes with cream; shaped and glazed.

Pommes de terre nouvelles. New potatoes.

Pommes de terre parisienne.
Potato balls rolled in a meat glaze and sprinkled with parsley.

Pommes de terre Parmentier.
Sautéed diced potatoes.

Pommes de terre persillées.
Boiled potatoes rolled in melted butter and parsley.

Pommes de terre en purée. Mashed potatoes.

Pommes de terre rissolées. Roast potatoes.

Pommes de terre en robe des champs.
Potatoes baked in the jacket.

Pommes de terre sautées. Sautéed potatoes.

Pommes de terre soufflées.
Very light whipped potatoes.

Pommes de terre surprise. Baked, stuffed potatoes.

VEGETABLES AND VEGETABLE DISHES
RICE AND NOODLE DISHES

Abbatis au riz. Giblets with rice.

Artichauts à la grecque.
Artichokes cooked in herbs and olive oil; usually served cold.

Asperges au gratin.
Asparagus in a rich creamy cheese sauce and buttered bread crumbs.

Asperges vinaigrette.
Asparagus with oil and vinegar.

Aubergine. Eggplant.

Aubergine farcie. Stuffed, baked eggplant.

Carottes flamandes. Creamed carrots.

Carottes glacées. Glazed carrots.

Céleri braisé. Braised celery.

Céleri rave.
Celery root served as a hot vegetable or a cold hors d'œuvre in a piquant sauce.

Cèpes à la moelle.
Mushrooms cooked with pieces of marrow.

Cèpes provençale.
Wild meaty mushrooms (bolitus variety) cooked with garlic and tomatoes.

Cèpes sautés à la provençale.
Sautéed mushrooms (bolitus variety) prepared with onions, garlic, tomatoes; provincial style.

Champignons. Small mushrooms.

Champignons farcis. Stuffed mushrooms.

Champignons grillés.
Mushrooms grilled in butter.

Chanterelles.   Type of mushroom.

Chou-au-lard.   Cabbage cooked with bacon.

Choucroute garnie.
Hot sauerkraut with meat and sausage.

Chou-fleur à l'huile.
Cauliflower marinated in oil and vinegar; served cold.

Chou de Bruxelles.   Brussels sprouts.

Choux farcis.   Stuffed cabbage.

Cœur de céleri.   Hearts of celery.

Concombre.   Cucumber.

Coquilletes.   Elbow macaroni.

Courgettes niçoise.   Squash with onions and rice.

Endive au jus.   Sautéed endive.

Endive au meunière.   Endive baked in butter.

Épinards en branche.,   Spinach cooked in butter.

Épinards à la crème.   Creamed spinach.

Flageolets.   Small kidney beans.

Fonds d'artichauts.   Hearts of artichokes.

Girolle.   Variety of mushroom.

Haricots rouges au vin.
Red beans cooked in wine.

Haricots verts sautés.   Sautéed string beans.

Laitue paysanne.
Lettuce cooked with ham, onions and carrots.

Laitue de printemps braisée au bacon.
Braised lettuce with bacon.

Légumes panachés.   Mixed vegetables.

Macaroni au fromage.   Macaroni with cheese.

Macaroni au gratin.
Macaroni with Béchamel sauce, sprinkled with grated
cheese, melted butter and baked.

Macaroni à la Nantua.
Cooked macaroni mixed with crayfish, baked and served in a timbale or mold.

Macédoine de légumes.
Mixture of diced, fresh vegetables.

Nouilles au fromage.   Noodles and cheese.

Petits pois à la française.
Tiny peas cooked with butter, finely minced onion and lettuce.

Petits pois au jambon.
Peas with minced onion and ham.

Petits pois aux laitues.   Peas with lettuce.

Points d'asperges.   Tender, green asparagus tips.

Pois à la française.
Green peas cooked with onions and lettuce.

Purée des légumes.
Creamed preparation of finely chopped vegetables.

Purée St. Germain.   Creamed green peas.

Purée soubise.   Creamed onions.

Ratatouille.
Chopped eggplant, green peppers, tomatoes, onions, garlic and olive oil; a dish of Arabic origin.

Risotto à la turque.
Rice with saffron and tomatoes.

Riz à la créole.
Rice with tomatoes and pimentoes.

Riz à la grecque.
Cooked rice with chopped onion, peas, sweet red pepper and shredded lettuce.

Riz sauvage.   Wild rice.

Riz à la valencienne.
Rice, tomatoes, saffron, onion and shellfish.

Tomates farcies.   Stuffed tomatoes.

Tomates grillées.   Grilled whole tomatoes.

Tomates sautées à la provençale.

Seasoned sliced tomatoes sautéed in olive oil with garlic, garnished with parsley and bread crumbs and baked.

Truffes.

Type of fungus that thrives underground, considered a true delicacy.   Can be used as an hors d'œuvre or vegetable but more usually a garnish.

Truffes au champagne.

Truffles in champagne sauce; served in a pastry crust.

Truffes à la crème.

Truffles in rich cream sauce and brandy; served in light pastry crust.

SALADS

French salads are varied but quite simple in preparation.   Dressings are added in small quantities and garlic is used very sparingly; perhaps the secret of French salad excellence is that it is mixed directly before serving.

Salade de betterave.

Thinly sliced beet salad with finely chopped herbs.

Salade caprice.

Similar to a chef's salad; that is various kinds of lettuce with a julienne of tongue, ham, chicken and artichoke hearts.

Salade de céleri.   Hearts of celery.

Salade de chicorée aux tomates.

Chicory and tomato salad.

Salade de chou rouge.   Red cabbage salad.

Salade de chou.   Coleslaw.

Salade de concombres.
Thinly sliced cucumbers with oil, vinegar and chervil.

Salade de cresson.   Watercress salad.

Salade cressonnière.
Salad mixture of potatoes, watercress, parsley, chervil
and hard-boiled egg.

Salade d'haricots secs et de lentilles.
Haricot beans and lentil salad with thinly sliced onion.

Salade d'haricots verts.   String bean salad.

Salade italienne.
Assortment of raw or cooked vegetables with salami,
anchovies, olives and capers with mayonnaise
dressing.

Salade de laitue et betteraves.
Lettuce and beet root salad.

Salade de légumes.
Freshly cooked vegetable salad with oil and vinegar
dressing.

Salade de lentilles.
Salad of cold boiled lentils, well seasoned.

Salade niçoise.
Salad of string beans, diced potatoes, tomatoes, olives,
anchovies and hard-boiled eggs served with oil and
vinegar.

Salade panachée au cresson.
Mixed salad with watercress.

Salade de pissenlit.   Dandelion salad.

Salade de poireau.   Leek salad.

Salade de pommes de terre.   Potato salad.

Salade de romaine à l'estragon.
Salad of romaine lettuce with fresh tarragon.

Salade russe.
Mixture of cooked vegetables, ham, lobster; all cut julienne style and mixed with mayonnaise.

Salade de saison.   Salad of the season.

Salade de scarole aux fines herbes.
Escarole salad with finely chopped herbs.

Salade de tomates.
Sliced tomatoes served in a tasty mixture of oil, vinegar and herbs.

Salade verte.   Mixed green salad.

Saladier.   Salad bowl.

CHEESE

Beaufort de Savoie.
Similar to Swiss gruyere; made of cow's milk.

Bonvillois.   Soft, creamy white cheese.

Brie.
Round, flat, creamy white cheese; made with cow's milk.

Cabrion.   Goat's milk cheese.

Cachat.   Cheese made with ewe's milk in Provence.

Camembert.
Creamy, ripe cheese; made with cow's milk in Normandy.

Cantal.   Small, hard cheese; made in Auvergne.

Chabris.   Goat's milk cheese.

Chèvre.   Chèvreton.   Chevrotin.   Chevrotton.
Goat's milk cheese; made in many varieties, sizes and shapes.

Coulommiers.
Creamy, sharp cow's milk cheese; from the Île de France region.

Crème Chantilly. Creamy, mild dessert cheese.

Demi-sel.
Light cream cheese made with cow's milk.

Dreux. Soft-textured cheese made with cow's milk.

Emmenthal.
Gruyère cheese with holes; from the Emme valley.

Fontainebleau. Cream cheese.

Forez. Similar to Roquefort cheese.

Fromage blanc. Cottage cheese.

Fromage à la crème. Cream cheese.

Fromage de chèvre. Goat's milk cheese.

Fromage de Hollande.
Dutch cheese; usually refers to Edam.

Géromé. Sharp cheese made with cow's milk.

Marlieu. Round, mild, white cheese.

Neufchâtel. Mild, creamy cheese from Normandy.

Olivet. Soft cheese from Orléans.

Persillé. Similar to Roquefort.

Petit suisse. Cream cheese.

Pont l'Évêque. Semi-hard cheese from Normandy.

Port-du-Salut OR **Port-Salut.**
Soft, smooth cheese with distinctive flavor.

Providence. Similar to Port-du-Salut.

Reblochon.
Soft whole milk cheese; from the Loire valley.

Roquefort.
Sharp, pungent, blue-veined cheese made with ewe's milk, and well aged.

Septmoncel. Hard cheese similar to Roquefort.

Suisse. Swiss cheese.

Trouville. Similar to Pont l'Évêque.

Vendôme. Similar to Camembert.

DESSERTS

Africains.   Small dessert cookies.

Ananas au kirsch.
Pineapple steeped in kirsch brandy.

Assiette de friandises.
Assortment of fancy cookies.

Baba au rhum.   Light yeast cake soaked in rum.

Biscuits.
Biscuits or delicate cookies usually served with ice cream.

Bombe.
Mould of ice cream, whipped cream and fruit; or several flavors of ice cream combined.

Bugne.   Doughnut.

Café viennois.   Coffee ice cream with whipped cream.

Cerises jubilée.
Brandied cherries served aflame over ice cream.

Chantilly.   Whipped cream.

Charlotte Malakoff.
Rich, creamy dessert made with lady fingers, whipped cream and almonds.

Compote.   Stewed fruit in light syrup.

Cornet de glace.   Ice cream cone.

Corbeille de fruits.   Basket of fruit.

Coupe favorite.
Ice cream flavored with kirsch, garnished with whipped cream and strawberry purée.

Coupe glacée.
Ice cream topped with whipped cream; similar to the American sundae.

Coupe (St.) Jacques.
Ices or ice cream heaped with a macédoine of fresh fruit in kirsch.

Crème caramel.   Light caramel cream pudding.

Crème Chantilly.   Whipped cream with sugar.

Crêpes au sucre.   Thin pancakes served with sugar.

Crêpes Suzette.
Thin pancakes steeped in a sauce made with butter, sugar, oranges, liqueurs and brandy, flamed in a chafing dish.

Café liégeois.
Coffee ice cream with whipped cream.

Dartois.
Cake made of light puff pastry usually filled with pastry cream or jelly.

Diplomate.
Cold pudding made with crushed fruit and whipped cream.

Doigt de dame.   Meringue lady fingers.

Éclair.   Éclair filled with whipped cream or custard.

Éclair au café.   Coffee éclair.

Éclair au chocolat.   Chocolate éclair.

Fraises à la crème.
Fresh strawberries served with sugar and cream.

Fraises des bois.
Small very fresh wild strawberries.

Fraises Romanoff.
Strawberries steeped in orange juice and curaçao with ice cream or whipped cream.

Framboises.   Fresh wild raspberries.

Fruits frais.   Fresh fruit.

Galette bretonne.
Round, flat tasty cookie made in Brittany.

Gâteau.
Cake. Gâteau de maison is the cake specialty of the house.

Gâteau d'amande.   Almond cake.

Génoise.
Smooth-textured yellow cake used for petits fours and sponge rolls.

Glace.   Ice cream or ices.

Glace à la vanille.   Vanilla ice cream.

Glace au chocolat.   Chocolate ice cream.

Glace aux fraises.   Strawberry ice cream.

Glace aux fruits.
Ice cream with crushed fruit or fruit syrup.

Glace napolitaine.   Combination of ices and ice cream.

Glace panachée.   Mixed ice cream.

Granité.   Ices with fruit syrup.

Liégeois.   Soft ice cream dessert.

Macédoine de fruits.
Mixture of fresh fruits and liqueur.

Madeleine.   Small butter cookie.

Marignan.   Sponge cake filled with whipped cream.

Marquise.   Ices with whipped cream.

Marrons glacés.   Candied chestnuts.

Massepain.
Colorful and decorative candy-like cookies made with almonds, sugar, eggs and flavoring.

Mazarin.
Yeast cake with kirsch brandy and sabayon sauce.

Melba.
Dessert sauce made with raspberries, currant jelly, lemon juice and sugar.

Melon glacé.   Cold melon.

Melon frappé.   Iced melon with liqueur.

Meringue.   Confection of egg whites and sugar.

Meringue glacée.
Ice cream in a swirl of baked egg white.

Mille-feuille.
Flaky puff pastry used as a tart or for cookies.

Mirabelles.   Small yellow plums.

Moka.   Pastry with mocha cream frosting.

Mont Blanc.
Fruit or chestnut purée with flavored whipped cream.

Mousse.
Light sweet dessert made with whipped cream and lightly beaten eggs.

Mousse au chocolat.   Chocolate mousse.

Mousse de fraises.   Strawberry mousse.

Napoléon.
Whipped cream or light custard sandwiched between flaky layers of delicate pastry.

Nesselrode.
Sauce or tart filling made with brandied fruits and chestnuts in a rich syrup.

Nougat.
Confection of almonds, pistachio nuts, honey and sugar.

Omelette flambée au rhum.
Omelet served with flamed rum sauce and powdered sugar.

Parfait.
Any combination of ice cream, whipped cream, fruits served in a tall glass.

Pâtisserie.   General term for pastry.

Pêche Melba.
Vanilla ice cream with peaches and crushed raspberry syrup.

Petit sablé.   Cookies.

Petits fours.
Small cakes or cookies.

Petits pots de crème.
Cold custard dessert prepared in many different flavors and served in small traditional French crocks.

Poire cardinal.
Stewed pears with raspberry sauce and toasted almonds.

Poire Hélène.
Stewed pears with vanilla ice cream and chocolate sauce.

Pomme au beurre.   Baked apple.

Pomme bonne femme.   Baked apple.

Pot au crème.
Custard dessert served in traditional crock.

Pouding.   Pudding.

Profiterole.
Small, flaky pastry filled with custard, ice cream or whipped cream usually served with chocolate sauce.

Pudding de cabinet.
Pudding made with candied fruits, raisins, liqueur and lady fingers.

Pudding de riz.   Rice pudding.

Pudding soufflé.
Light, fluffy pudding made with stiffly beaten egg whites.

Riz impératrice.
Rice pudding with candied fruit and whipped cream; served cold.

Sablés.   Small, tasty cookies.

Savarin.
Rum-soaked sponge cake served with fruit and garnished with whipped cream.

Sorbet.   Sherbet.

Soufflé.
Egg yolks, stiffly beaten whites and an extensive variety of fruit, flavors, syrups are the basic ingredients for a favorite dessert or entrée. Served cold or hot and sometimes flamed.

Soufflé au chocolat.   Chocolate soufflé.

Soufflé aux liqueurs.
Soufflé flavored distinctively with a particular liqueur.

Soufflé à la vanille.   Vanilla soufflé.

Stanislas.   Cake with almond cream filling.

Tarte.   Open pastry shell filled with fruit or custard.

Tarte aux fraises.   Strawberry tart.

Tartelettes.   Little tarts filled with fruit or custard.

Tranche napolitaine.
Ice cream slice of several flavors.

Tranche plombières.   Ice cream with fruit.

Vacherin.   Meringue shell filled with whipped cream.

Yaourt.   Yogurt.

BEVERAGES

Cacoa.   Cocoa.

Café.   Coffee.

Café brûlot.   Coffee with sugar and flaming brandy.

Café complet.
Refers to continental breakfast consisting of coffee with hot milk, rolls, jam and butter.

Café crème.   Coffee with cream.

Café diable.
Coffee with cinnamon, cloves, sugar, orange rind and flaming brandy.

Café double.   Double-strength coffee.

Café filtre.   Strong drip coffee.

Café frappé OR **glacé.**   Iced coffee.

Café au lait.   Coffee with hot milk.

Café nature OR **noir.**   Black coffee.

Café soluble.   Instant coffee.

Orange pressé.   Fresh fruit orangeade.

Thé.   Tea.

INDEX

The words in capitals refer to sections, and the number that follows (example: p. 81) refers to the page. Otherwise, ALL ENTRIES ARE INDEXED BY ITEM NUMBER.

LISTEN & LEARN CASSETTES

Complete, practical at-home language learning courses for people with limited study time—specially designed for travelers.

Special features:

* Dual-language—Each phrase first in English, then the foreign-language equivalent, followed by a pause for repetition (allows for easy use of cassette even without manual).

* Native speakers—Spoken by natives of the country who are language teachers at leading colleges and universities.

* Convenient manual—Contains every word on the cassettes—all fully indexed for fast phrase or word location.

Each boxed set contains one 90-minute cassette and complete manual.

Listen & Learn French .... Cassette and Manual
99914-9 $8.95

Listen & Learn German .... Cassette and Manual
99915-7 $8.95

Listen & Learn Italian............................. Cassette and Manual
99916-5 $8.95

Listen & Learn Japanese......................... Cassette and Manual
99917-3 $8.95

Listen & Learn Modern Greek .... Cassette and Manual
99921-1 $8.95

Listen & Learn Modern Hebrew .... Cassette and Manual
99923-8 $8.95

Listen & Learn Portuguese...................... Cassette and Manual
99919-X $8.95

Listen & Learn Russian .... Cassette and Manual
99920-3 $8.95

Listen & Learn Spanish........................... Cassette and Manual
99918-1 $8.95

Listen & Learn Swedish .... Cassette and Manual
99922-X $8.95

Precise, to-the-point guides for adults with limited learning time

ESSENTIAL GRAMMAR SERIES

Designed for independent study or as supplements to conventional courses, the *Essential Grammar* series provides clear explanations of all aspects of grammar—no trivia, no archaic material. Do not confuse these volumes with abridged grammars. These volumes are complete.

ESSENTIAL FRENCH GRAMMAR, Seymour Resnick. Includes 2500 item cognate list. 159pp. 5⅜ × 8½.
·20419-7 Pa. $2.75

ESSENTIAL GERMAN GRAMMAR, Guy Stern and E. F. Bleiler. Unusual shortcuts on noun declension, word order. 124pp. 5⅜ × 8½.
·20422-7 Pa. $2.95

ESSENTIAL ITALIAN GRAMMAR, Olga Ragusa. Includes useful discussion of verb idioms essential in Italian. 111pp. 5⅜ × 8½.
·20779-X Pa. $2.95

ESSENTIAL JAPANESE GRAMMAR, E. F. Bleiler. In Romaji, no characters needed. Japanese grammar is regular and simple. 156pp. 5⅜ × 8½.
21027-8 Pa. $2.95

ESSENTIAL PORTUGUESE GRAMMAR, Alexander da R. Prista. Includes 4 appendices covering regular, irregular verbs. 114pp. 5⅜ × 8½.
21650-0 Pa. $3.50

ESSENTIAL SPANISH GRAMMAR, Seymour Resnick. Includes 2500 word cognate list. 115pp. 5⅜ × 8½.
·20780-3 Pa. $2.75

ESSENTIAL ENGLISH GRAMMAR, Philip Gucker. Combines modern functional and traditional approaches. 177pp. 5⅜ × 8½.
21649-7 Pa. $3.50

·Not available in British Commonwealth Countries except Canada.